Taking the High Road

How to Cope with Your Ex-Husband, Maintain Your Sanity, and Raise Your Child in Peace

NAILAH SHAMI

A PLUME BOOK

PLUME
Published by the Penguin Group
Penguin Putnam Inc., 375 Hudson Street,
New York, New York 10014, U.S.A.
Penguin Books Ltd, 27 Wrights Lane, London W8 5TZ, England
Penguin Books Australia Ltd, Ringwood, Victoria, Australia
Penguin Books Canada Ltd, 10 Alcorn Avenue,
Toronto, Ontario, Canada M4V 3B2
Penguin Books (N.Z.) Ltd, 182–190 Wairau Road,
Auckland 10, New Zealand

Penguin Books Ltd, Registered Offices:
Harmondsworth, Middlesex, England

First published by Plume,
a member of Penguin Putnam Inc.

First Printing, January, 2000
10 9 8 7 6 5 4 3 2 1

 REGISTERED TRADEMARK—MARCA REGISTRADA

LIBRARY OF CONGRESS CATALOGING-IN-PUBLICATION DATA:
Shami, Nailah.
    Taking the high road : how to cope with your ex-husband,
maintain your sanity, and raise your child in peace / Nailah Shami.
        p. cm.
    Includes bibliographical references.
    ISBN 0-452-28155-5
    1. Divorced mothers.   2. Divorced people—Family relationships.
3. Children of divorced parents—Family relationships.   I. Title.
HQ814.S447   2000
306.89—dc21   99-38572
                                                 CIP

Printed in the United States of America
Set in Garamond Light

to Esprit

ACKNOWLEDGMENTS

From the sweetest place in my heart, I'd like to acknowledge the following:

To my Esprit, thank you for keeping me humble and for making this a "living" book. For the lessons, the love, the trust, and for providing most of the fake names in the book.

To my king, Imhotep, Merlin had nothing on you. Your magic and laughter have been both a shield and a feather bed. Thanks for keeping it juicy, and *real*, and for showing me so many more sides of love than I knew before you.

To Alma, for warming my hands, my feet . . . my soul, and for loving me through valleys and peaks. Welcome to the meadow, girl.

To my "twin towers," my brothers Joe and Sonny, for care packages of incense, lavender oil, candles, African fabric to wrap my head, phone hugs; for being grand husbands, fathers, and uncles; and for always doing the hard things with a laugh. *I love you.*

To Janis Donnaud, my agent, for believing in me enough not to send me one of those ugly, "This-does-not-currently-suit-our-needs" letters when I mailed off the first draft of the manuscript, and for walking and talking the publishing houses of New York in my name. To Dutton, for saying "yes." To my editing angel, Jennifer Moore, for polishing my prose while honoring my voice. I didn't mean what I said about the chicken scratch.

To "O," for soft words, laughter, and unbound love.

viii   *ACKNOWLEDGMENTS*

To Anita, Jacqueline K., Brian C., Vivian M., Karen Z., and Sharon S., for cheering without details.

To my nephew Michael, I'm proud of you too. Keep writing.

To my cuddly ones, Malik, André, and Kamilah, for still being "so fresh from God."

To my Reiki family and all of the prayer warriors at Unity Church of Bellevue. You know why.

To Luther Vandross, Johnny Mathis, Gabrielle Roth, Nancy Wilson, Enya, Roberta Flack, and Yanni for providing the background music while I wrote.

To the teachings, writings, and productions that have inspired me: *Star Trek*, the Muppets, *Run for the Dream*, Milton Erickson, Carolyn Myss, Maya Angelou, Anne Lamott, Tony Robbins, Louise Hay, Oprah Winfrey, Merlin, *Peanuts*, *Webster's New Complete Thesaurus*, Rumi, and Dr. Seuss.

To everyone in this book who knowingly and unknowingly shared their stories with me, and to those who walk this path with us. *Hold on.* There's a rainbow at this end of this thing. *I swear.*

And to God, for watching over me while I grew.

CONTENTS

Taking the High Road

INTRODUCTION:
WHY THE HIGH ROAD?

"Let nothing come between you and the light."
—Thoreau

In the months following our separation, my ex-husband, who had been my best friend for a decade and a Hallmark father for seven years, became so pigheaded, wily, and entirely amnesiac about the promise he'd made to have a friendly divorce that I thought for sure we'd wind up on *Jerry Springer.* I briefly claimed emotional asylum in a divorce support group, with the hope that we could huddle, break, and then run screaming into the good days. But my wounded comrades had been tackled so many times that they just lay there waiting for a stretcher. Between them and my stack of "divorce" books, I was a walking encyclopedia of horror stories, grief, and warfare tactics . . . and a few referrals for hit men and sorcerers. Don't get me wrong—I could have paraded wounds with the best of them and flopped down for my stretcher rescue too, but I suck at Victim, even when it's true.

My fairy tale was to flip through the pages of my *Happily Divorced* scrapbook by firelight, knowing that we had ended our marriage but were still friends who were very committed to raising our little one together. It was my story—come to think of it, it was "our" story at one point—and I was sticking to it.

Unfortunately, he wasn't.

But I'm a stubborn little thing when it comes to preserving my fantasies, and since I'd already locked in on how I thought it should go, there would be no major plot changes. So, I decided to try to help him remember his role by becoming his divorce recovery sponsor. If that makes you want to roll on the floor and beat the rug, guess where I got most of my early intervention strategies? *Star Trek* and *Muppet Baby* marathons. I swear.

The multispecies *Star Trek* crew somehow always managed to beat off scarier-than-life adversaries and catastrophic cogs so they could soar through the galaxy another day. They inspired me to look beyond what might have normally been possible too. And Jim Henson's singing Muppets, God bless them, kept me innocent, and happy, while I worked.

Plucking practical, usable postdivorce tools from huge singing stuffed puppets and aliens is an acquired skill, and it took a special kind of patience, openness, and naïveté, but it was one of the most healing things I've ever done, much more enchanting than the marathon grief-vigil support group.

For a little over a year, under the guidance of Kermit, Gonzo, Miss Piggy, and a host of alien mentors, I masqueraded as a divorce recovery sponsor, which often included, but was not limited to, behavior modification therapy, spiritual counseling, and collections.

I was like a heat-seeking missile. My target was to find the "yes" in him. "Yes, I'll cooperate." "Yes, I'll behave." "Yes, I want to be happily-ever-after-divorced too."

Then I waited patiently for him to join me in the zone. Sometimes he did, but more often he planted detour signs around the zone and looped us both through the House of Horrors. Fangs, slime, glow-in-the-dark skeletons, and all.

Then one day, two years A.D. (after divorce), as I was fingering my list of lifetime goals—which I have an almost unnatural relationship with because I am a time-management fiend—I recalled a favorite saying of an old friend: "Time is precious, so be careful how you spend it, and with whom you spend it, because you can never get it back."

Sure I wanted Ex Charming, but shepherding his evolution was cutting into *my* time. Nowhere on that list did it say I was going to spend 20+ hours a week and some of my REM time apprenticing as a divorce recovery sponsor for the next decade. How was I going to get to the bazillion things on my list if I couldn't see past him?

So I gave it up. Sort of.

It was a three-step process. I went from a divorce recovery sponsor to the Get-Along-with-Your-Ex missionary to . . . well, you'll see.

Step 1: Me, the Divorce Recovery Sponsor

During my stint as divorce recovery sponsor, I sequestered myself for weeks at a time. No world or local news, no friends, no family, no church or novels. It wasn't until I broke trance that I noticed that the lives of my divorced coworkers, neighbors, churchmates, associates, etc. were downright sorry too.

Easy, friendly divorce seemed as challenging as trying to control the weather, but I seemed to be winging it a lot better than most of them. I might have been a wee bit disillusioned during my withdrawal from 24-7 Pollyanna mania, but the rest of the troupe was out of the box.

It's not that he had become Ex Charming or anything. He was still working my nerves, but at least I wasn't slashing his tires, sending anonymous, fragranced love letters that his new live-in girlfriend would have undoubtedly opened and suspiciously interrogated him about, telling Esprit he was descended from a swamp thing, or living on chocolate cherry cream decadence cake.

Step 2: Me, the Get-Along-with-Your-Ex Missionary

I started sharing my get-along tips with the more down-trodden to help them find some peace in their lives: Be decent, stay light, honor your children's right to have two "working" parents, and hold on long enough to tiptoe through the anger, hurt, ambiguity, and disappointment *anyway.*

This was my rallying charge when I began National Get Along with Your Ex Month (NGAWYEM) in 1997, a month-long campaign designed to inspire divorced parents with children to behave themselves for the month of July. Step 1 was taking the NGAWYEM pledge:

> "Although I am no longer in a committed relationship with my child's other parent, I will make every effort to be a good ex and to maintain a working relationship with him/her for the sake of our child.
>
> "I promise to be a person of honor and character, taking the high road as often as possible, even when I don't feel like it, and regardless of how my ex behaves. I swear."

Mothers took it. Fathers took it. Friends, family, attorneys, and counselors requested packets for bickering couples they knew. Splinter groups formed. One woman who called the campaign line even told me that she ran across a packet of NGAWYEM information in her divorce judge's waiting room.

My ex, whom I shared the information with, said it was a good idea, you know . . . nod . . . for those people who are, you know . . . troubled, but he never gave me back his registration slip.

Carrying out the NGAWYEM pledge was a no-brainer for pledgers with exes-you-wondered-why-they'd-divorced-in-the-first-place or exes-who-would-rather-eat-worms-all-day-every-day-than-live-with-their-formers-again-but-were-still-willing-to-meet-them-on-the-high-road-for-the-kids'-sake (let's call these folks the A's). But for pledgers with exes with an attitude (we'll call these poor souls the B's), walking the pledge walk was like trying to have a meaningful conversation with an ant.

After two years of calls, letters, and e-mail from both A's and B's, I'm here to tell you that if you're an A, you're living large. Break out the sparkling cider, and pass this book on to any B you know.

A's had an occasional, situational explosion once . . . every five years, but B's were stranded in the land mine belt.

B's were parents with exes who were generally year-round deadbeats, boneheads, bullies, manipulators, situational Neanderthals, and experts at self-induced multiple personality disorder who loved to bark orders and insults and instigate.

B's were women like Cherise, whose husband left her for the next-door neighbor and then barbecued in the front yard every weekend with his new honey and who paid for remodeling their love shack instead of child support.

They were women like Nona, whose two small children returned from Dad's house every other weekend singsonging things like "Mommy's a nut. Mommy's a nut."

They were women like 30-year-old Bettice, whose ex picked their children up from her sister's every Friday for visitation. Then he hung around at Sis's for an hour, bashing Bettice all the while.

My basic intervention fell short with them.

Was I supposed to tell any one of them to focus on the greater good, pull out their pledge cards, recite them 100 times, review the "How to Be a Good Pledge" tip sheet, and pull themselves together with a straight face? Especially Cherise, who had bipolar disorder and therefore might have had a medical alibi for slinking next door while her ex and his new honey were cuddling in the hammock, tipping the barbecue over, and burning their house to the ground?

Step 3: Me, the Goddess

On and on went the battle-weary Ripley's stories—which got more believable with each phone call—and the little-dingers compilations from these dutiful scouts who were co-parenting A.D. with someone who thought the pledge was a joke.

They didn't have the fairy tale divorce either, nor a calling to be divorce recovery sponsors. And trying to get along was lopsided and unfulfilling as a sole coping tool. They also wanted to get over, get through it, and get on with their lives without looking like the "before" version of Ebenezer Scrooge. And some of them wanted to know what kind of happy pills I was taking.

I didn't have a label for this "state" they craved, this thing they thought I had and could transfuse, until I had an interview with Stephanie Shapiro of the *Baltimore Sun* during the 1998 NGAWYEM campaign.

As fate would have it, Esprit's dad called before the interview to tell me that he had left $50 for Esprit at her middle school to cover her graduation dress (a dress I had told her we couldn't afford). Either he said, or I imagined him following it up with, "Nannee, nannee, nannee." I was overcome by a horrible case of brain sore just wondering how he, who was seven months in arrears with child support, would think it was okay to gift Esprit $50.

But I wrestled my heckler alter ego to the ground and gagged her before she could blurt out, "Hey, who's holding your brain right now, and when are you going to go pick it up?" Then, with tears in my eyes that I'm grateful he couldn't see, I calmly told him I was going to garnishee the money, lump it into the household budget, and deduct it from the arrears, but he was still welcome to come to her graduation. He called me a blurpee, blurpee, blurpee control freak and hung up.

I slapped the heckler before she had a chance to hit *69.

Sad as it was, after I helped her up, I spent two whole minutes trying to figure out if I really was a blurpee, blurpee, blurpee control freak. And although I was hardly in the mood for it, I was scheduled to do a phone interview with Stephanie 13 minutes later.

For the first six minutes, I practiced faking the Indian accent I was going to use to tell Stephanie she had the wrong number when the phone rang. Then I took several long, slow breaths, massaged my ears and my jaw, and recited the pledge about 50 times. I really did. Then I pictured Cherise, Nona, and Bettice, and all the new B pledgers I'd talked to that week.

How was I ever going to face them again if I went back and edited the second part of the pledge—

"I promise to be a person of honor and character, taking the high road as often as possible, even when I don't feel like it, and regardless of how my ex behaves. I swear."

—to read:

"I'll try to be a person of honor and character, except when my ex acts like a butt. When he does, I'll take it personally, and melt down. I swear."

The phone rang. It was Stephanie.
Guess what her third question was?
"Do you have any bitter feelings toward your ex when he behaves badly?"
Really.
Seeing how I'd just had fresh, live slime lobbed on me 13 minutes ago, maybe it wasn't the time to ask. Or maybe it was? It was the question that consciously moved me to share step 3 of my transition.

I reeled through the conversation I'd just had with him and some of my other dubious experiences A.D. and softly said, "I'm human. Ugly stuff hurts. But I can have all the feelings in the world and still remain graceful for my daughter's sake and for mine.

"I owe my ex a lot, so if I was to call him anything, it would be *sensei*. His ineptitude and ugliness have forced me to fully realize my gifts. In the process, I have become a goddess and I have to thank him for that. I have to. If not for him, there are amazing things I would not be."

Now when you say something like that to the press, or, for that matter, to anyone who has not had that divine experience of embracing and celebrating the threads of her power and possibility, who does not get it, you have to be prepared for dead space, laughter, or having your file marked "Wannabe Messiah."

Out of context, it sounds like a cross between something an utterly narcissistic, big-time diva and a devoted monk who's been in the Andean mountains for 10 years waiting for enlightenment would say, doesn't it? Out of context, it sounds like I go around all the time with my nose in the air acting like I own the Nile and a string of planets.

But in context, it means, "There may be slime on my slippers at the moment, but it doesn't belong there, so I'm going to wipe it off because I'm on my way to a dance."

I told Stephanie about the phone call. I told her I had exactly 40 minutes to wrap up the interview because I was going to pick up my daughter from school for dinner and a movie. After that, boxercise class. Then I had a date with my heated, vibrating foot bath.

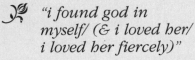

"i found god in
myself/ (& i loved her/
i loved her fiercely)"

—NTOZAKE SHANGE

When I read her article a week later, I cheered Stephanie for not writing me off as a somewhat bigheaded, New Age loon and canceled the order with the phone company to change my number. The headline for the article might as well have read "CALLING ALL GODDESSES and Wannabes," because that's who rang.

Each had a gremlin at her front door, and she was desperately seeking sanity, solutions, and hope. Get along? How can I? And where are you getting those happy pills? You've never met my ex, but I promise you he's one of the evil misfits in Stephen King's latest novel. How do you get to goddess in the midst of that?

You, the Goddess

You can copycat my long, yellow-brick-road route to goddess, but I'd recommend a straight jump. It's a big word, I know, and it's also a big, wonderful place to start the first day of the rest of your life with co-parenting with Pooh-bah.

This is not a religious proposition, so I don't expect you to go around blessing anyone. Supernatural powers are not included. *American Heritage* defines "goddess" as "a woman of great beauty or grace," and that's what you will be. And don't worry, after you become a goddess, your hat size will remain the same. But, if you still don't like the word "goddess," substitute another one you think is synonymous with "all that!"

If, after that, you still think the ego police are going to hop out of the closet, stamp the word "DIVA" on your forehead, and make you write "I must be more humble" 500 times, let me ask you this final question to help peel your hands off the safety rail.

How many seconds does it usually take for you to decide you're something scandalous, like, say, the "B" word?

Why would you let it take any longer than that to get to goddess?

Are you with me?

> *"God respects us when we work but loves us when we dance."* —Old Sufi saying

How to Get the Most out of This Book

Taking the High Road was born in the same hole in which I buried my "divorce recovery sponsor" shingle. But a lot of my early wizardry actually made my ex a more palatable soul. My wand-waving days or the refinement of my inner spirit and goddess philosophy—how could I tell you that one more than the other brought me here? So I will share the whole wave with you. Take what you need.

My goal is to help you develop more resourceful emotions and behaviors—patience, power, joy, creativity, and humor, to name a few—so you can get along with, get over, and get through life with your difficult ex, while taking care of yourself and your children.

We're going to step through this process together, strategizing and laughing all the way, and then we're not going to talk about it anymore because it won't be an issue. Okay?

You will get the most out of this journey if you:

1. Believe it can change your life.
2. Read the whole book.
3. Do the exercises and visualizations, even if you think they're strange. They're designed to help to gently recondition your mind so you can interact with your ex in more positive ways.
4. Transfer the affirmations to index cards. They can be incredibly calming by themselves. Pick one or two

suitable affirmations and repeat them aloud all day, until you feel better.

5. Put these ideas to work for you for the next 90 days.

You might not find a personalized psychic prescription for every problem you're having with your ex in this book (difficult exes come in many strains), but read closely and you will gather enough "starter" strands to weave your own high road strategies as needed. As you develop a wider range of responses in difficult situations, your ability to maneuver will increase, and you will begin to interact with your ex in new ways.

What should your first step be? It's simple:

Stop doing anything you've been doing that hasn't worked, and faithfully try each technique in the book for at least 90 days. (Yes, you can use more than one at a time.) If something doesn't work for you after 90 days of *regular practice,* then *stop doing it* and try something else.

Take what does work and use it until it becomes second nature. Sometimes you will have to make an external shift and change the circumstance. Sometimes you will have to make an inner shift and change your attitude or your expectations. Do whatever it takes. Then share it with another person who might benefit. This will not only help you perfect the skill but also empower another person.

In the beginning, certain taunting, six-year-old, sabotage questions may pop into your head, such as:

"Why do I have to be good, when my ex is acting like the fool?"

You don't have to. You can do what my favorite 3-year-old, Kamilah, does when she doesn't want to do something. You can scream "No, no, no, boo, no!" while you're running down the hallway.

You can go back to LIFE AS IS anytime. But if you want things to change, you have to change things.

"What the caterpillar calls the end of the world, the master calls a butterfly." —Richard Bach, *Illusions*

Reach for the Dream, and You'll Be the Winner

If I were there with you now, I would take your hands in mine and ask you to tuck this secret into your palms while you're turning the pages of this book:

All of this is for you and your child.

The character, grace, honor, and humor you show now will help you reduce the frequency and intensity of "domestic terrorism," your reaction to it and recovery time for both you and your child. It will help you develop and maintain more resourceful emotions and behaviors. Your ex will benefit too, but this is a good thing, and it will come back to you.

Can gremlin exes be permanently rehabilitated? I don't know, and I really don't care anymore. But I care about you and your children, and I believe you can create a wonderful life.

This seven-year collection of tips, affirmations, reflections, rituals, and prayers have helped me stay calm, measured, and powerful through some of the worst days of my life, and maintain the spirit, passion, magic, and joy that I needed to dance down the streets again, and sleep through the night. With all my heart, I hope they will do the same for you.

I challenge you to do whatever it takes to get on the high road and stay there.

Put the ideas in this book to work for you right away, and use them over and over until the picture changes. *Live them.* Because it makes no difference what you know if you are not willing to live it. And I promise you that if you have that kind of integrity, the road will rise to meet you.

May the blessings be.

Nailah

NOTE:

Physical threats and abuse are beyond the scope of this book. If your ex is violent or mentally ill, please contact the police and seek legal restraints.

❧ PART 1 ❧

Tools for the Road

> "On the day of liberation when you look back at your life, you will laugh and laugh and laugh. Why not laugh and laugh now." —Ramana Maharshi

Shortly after my divorce, my friend Hamadi said something to me one night while I was blubbering into the phone that sounded so vague and useless at the time that I swore I'd call my old army drill sergeant for comfort before I called him again.

But the more I thought about what he'd said over the next few days, the more his no-nonsense command seemed like a prophetic revelation, and the more I regretted having whited his number out of my phone book. He said:

"Do whatever it takes to get through this and still be you."

A High Roader's Dozen

1. Turn this into an opportunity.
2. Map out your sanity plan.
3. Do the work.
4. Lean toward easy
5. Be your own fairy godmother.
6. Shower yourself with TLC.
7. Learn to playact.
8. Keep your perspective.
9. Reduce your ex cooties.
10. Cancel the pity party and drop that voodoo doll.
11. Lean on those who love you.
12. Focus, focus, focus.

1. Turn This into an Opportunity

> *"We should be careful to get out of an experience all the wisdom that is in it."* —Samuel L. Clemens

You prayed for Ex Charming, I'm sure—I did—but like you I got Grand Pooh-bah Pain in the Butt, who was like a hybrid of the Tasmanian Devil and Godzilla and appeared to be psychically engineered to locate and sever my last nerve. No one could have told me when he first showed up on my doorstep that he was really here to help me become a stronger person, a better me. As unbelievable as it may seem, that's what your Pooh-bah is here to do for you too.

Nevertheless, after a brief initial performance, I had more than a fleeting notion of hopping on an undisclosed red-eye flight out of town and starting life over under an assumed identity. I was going to be Maria, the lantern maker, and Esprit, Carol Sue, my divine conception. But I couldn't finance the move, and I realized that Carol Sue would never have forgiven me for separating her from her daddy and giving her two first names. So I prayed for deliverance. I prayed for strength.

I had his daughter. Divorced or not, he was going to keep showing up for the next 11 years, and I wanted to find a way to live through it. I woke up the next morning with my instructions.

Just hang on, baby. He's here to teach you something.

I sat up in bed feeling gypped, feeling like God should have really been doing stand-up. *Hang on?* Please.

Back down under the covers with Reiki (my teddy bear), I slunked, hoping God was just pausing. Nothing else came, but the more I nestled with Reiki, the more I glumly conceded that all the Pooh-bahs before him had, in fact, been my great teachers. Irritating, but motivating.

So I grumbled a "thank you" to God, as I always do on dubious delivery, and put in dibs on a kinder, gentler evolution next time. Then I went on about my day, and the next few months, and the next few years—even though there was no visible evidence of it—pretending Pooh-bah's antics had some divine purpose.

Too much pretending can land you in a special little room in a state mental compound with a bunkmate who believes she has an invisible lizard tail. But a pinch here and there can smooth out ex cooties.

I want you to put your book down in a minute and make a list of all the behaviors your ex does that make you want to drape a gunnysack over his head and drop him off at the zoo. Next, I want you to pretend that each of these behaviors can help you become a better you.

Close your eyes, take a few deep breaths, and link up each bad-boy behavior with a benefit. It might help to imagine yourself as a contestant on *High Road Jeopardy!* The category you've chosen is *How My Ex's Crazy Behavior Can Help Me Grow as a Human Being.*

If your ex is constantly late picking up the kids, for instance, your *High Road Jeopardy!* solution could be to become more assertive or more patient if he's just a few minutes off. So your question would be: *"What is becoming more assertive or more patient?"*

Let's try another one.

What if he refers to you as fatso to mutual friends? Then your *High Road Jeopardy!* question might go something like this: *"What is learning to blow off things that don't really matter?"*

Take about 15 minutes now to write down all the possibilities, all of the opportunities that await you. *Do not read another word until you've done that.*

Now, if that was really, really hard, you need remedial

pretending. Try *High Road Jeopardy!* again, using these crib notes.

1. What is learning how to handle grossly difficult people so that not one of them can ever ruin my day again?
2. What is learning to put things back together that would blow poor little Humpty-Dumpty's mind?
3. What is learning to laugh when nothing seems funny?
4. What is learning to become a revolving source of inspiration for myself and others?
5. What is learning to manage my emotions, keeping the positive ones on top?
6. What is learning to be a zillion times more resourceful?
7. What is learning to become a masterful communicator?

If you get stuck, try harder. You *can* do this.

Sometimes we can get so trapped in the pain, we cannot see where a thing is taking us. Pooh-bah may be Poohbah, but you can decide where it's going to take you.

Affirmations

1. Lessons come from everywhere.
2. I trust that this experience will deliver me to a richer life.
3. I am willing to grow through this.

2. MAP OUT YOUR
SANITY PLAN

There are times when Pooh-bah will make you want to suck your thumb. But, as a goddess-in-training, you can develop a set of strategies to keep you in control no matter how unruly he gets. The key is to be prepared. First, we're going to create your master sanity plan, so go get a big sheet of paper.

Label the first side "Him" and the second "Me."

Now, ask yourself what it would be like if your ex was a model co-parent and you didn't really need this book? Picture him in his new, good-guy skin—during visitation, phone conversations, interactions with your child, paying child support, and any other situations where you'd like to see his behavior improve. What is he saying? How is he behaving? How does he look? How do you feel?

Stuff reality into a glass jar for now and stick it under the sink. It's your piece of paper, live large. Now, before the censor in you kicks it, describe your fantasy ex on the "Him" side in present tense (for example, "he is polite," "he is tactful in front of our daughter," "he pays child support on time and in full," "he civilly discusses concerns about her development and welfare," "he picks her up and brings her back on time"). Once you're done with the "Him" list, imagine what it would be like if he doesn't change a lick. Or what if, heaven forbid, he turns into Pooh-bah, the Second Coming. What behaviors and mind-sets will help you survive him?

Me List Examples

I keep my cool around him at all times.

I am very relaxed when I'm talking to him about difficult subjects.

I am willing to work at maintaining a working relationship for our child's sake.

I am pleasant whether he is or not.

I am at peace when he comes to pick up our child.

I am able to laugh with him.

I am a goddess.

Now, scratch everything off the "Me" list that makes you want to scream "Liar, liar, pants on fire!" and anything that you are not willing to put time into right now. When you have 1 to 10 items left, copy them to the blanks below; put the things you value most first. (You can work on the others later.)

1. _____

2. _____

3. _____

4. _____

5. _____

6. _____

7. _____

8. _____

9. _____

10. _____

Transfer your "Me" list to two identical index cards. Keep one card before you as you embrace the ideas in the rest of this book and make choices about how you are going to behave for the next 90 days. Put the other card on your nightstand or tape it to your bedroom mirror and review it every morning and every night. It will keep you focused on where you want to go. So will the next exercise.

Imagine that it's a year from now, and everything on your "Me" list is true. A mother who has chosen you as her mentor is interviewing you. Tell her what you did to transform your relationship with your ex and what it means to you. Record your testimonial below.

My Relationship with My Ex
This Time Next Year

What I Did to Transform My Relationship with My Ex

1. I finished *Taking the High Road,* and put the ideas to work in my life.

2. _____

   _____

   _____

3. _____

   _____

   _____

4. _____

_____

_____

5. _____

_____

_____

What It Means to Me

_____

_____

_____

_____

_____

Two Steps Ahead

You cannot prepare for every ex-plosion—Pooh-bahs are notoriously unpredictable—but you can diffuse so many of them that the ones that slip through won't make you want to suck your thumb.

One of the best ways to stay a few steps ahead of your ex is lifescaping—intently dwelling on the status of your life in regularly designated stints and coming up with ideas that will help you live the life you want. You can start lifescaping by setting aside one hour a week to toss around the following brainstorming categories:

1. What's coming up?
2. What are my priorities?
3. How can I handle potential trouble spots?
4. What can I do this week to accomplish what I consider most important?
5. What do I *want* to do this week?

Lifescaping shouldn't stress you. Do it in your favorite lounge chair, on a walk, in the tub, or lying in bed. The point is for you to spend focused but relaxed time reflecting on your life and the way you want it to flow. If you keep a running list of your priorities, goals, and strategies, they will guide you.

Use 10 of your lifescaping minutes on your ex (we'll talk more about this time limit later on). The cheat sheet on page 25 will help you chart habitually naughty behaviors he might demonstrate in the next week and brainstorm about how you can put a plug in them, so you can get back to the things on your "Me" list. Return to this section when you find techniques you want to try, jot them down in the margin, and then implement them shortly before, or during, the anticipated behavior.

Give your strategies some time to work, but not forever. A day is a too-short test period, and one year is too long. Anything you decide on in between is fine. In general, 90 days is reasonable turnaround time for behavior modification, but more deep-seated habits may require more dismantling time, so you gauge.

If it doesn't work after a reasonable time, *try something else*.

Here is a section from NGAWYEM pledger Janet's cheat sheet:

Behavior

Makes demeaning comments
when he comes to pick up
the children

Strategies

1. Witnessing (page 43)
2. Invite friends over on
   pickup days
   (page 131)
3. Have him pick up
   the children from
   school
4. Repeat affirmations
   and prayers

Behavior

Picks children up late

Strategies

1. Blow it off
2. Request that he
   come on time or
   reschedule (use the
   Pooh-bah Power
   Talk model in Chap-
   ter 16)
3. Make other plans for
   the children

Affirmations

1. I care so much about how my days are going to turn
   out that I make plans.
2. I am willing to be powerful.
3. I choose to create my life with a purpose.
4. I can change my life at any moment.
5. I am willing to believe in things I cannot see.

3. Do the Work

The transformation of your relationship with your ex won't happen without you. You may start begrudgingly at first, like a doubting Thomasina even, but soon enough your effort and your grace will pay off. For a while, I thought getting along with Pooh-bah meant I had to always be in some really enthusiastic, loving, passionate, hyped-up, altered, "led" state—like Pollyanna on LSD (and sometimes I was)—but on many mornings during those early days, I woke up hungover from cynicism, feeling whipped and heartbroken.

Every day that first month, I fantasized about volunteering to be a participant in the new antidepressant medication study at a local hospital. Every time the radio ad came on I wrote the number down.

My immune system surrendered unconditionally. I lost 10 pounds, got my first cold in years, had a running bladder infection, and I was so grossly anemic at one point that the blood bank rejected my blood. I still remember the sweet little nurse coming back with my pitiful hemoglobin count from the funny machine they spin your blood in to see if it's worth taking. When she took my hand, she had a sympathetic look in her eyes that said, "I wish I could give you a takeout transfusion right here." Then she sent me to my doctor for iron supplements.

Looking back on it now, I may have needed those experimental antidepressant drugs they kept mentioning on the radio to chase down my iron pills. Maybe you think you do too.

But maybe you don't. How will you know unless you

play it out? How will you know unless you allow yourself to show up and work your way down your list like it's all you have to do in the world?

Emotion doesn't matter right now, behavior does. You can have the blues like you've never had them before, and be semihomicidal on top of that, and still do this work. It all may seem very simple and one-dimensional to you, but this is the juice that runs through a winner's heart. Winners show up. Winners do the work.

If you do this day after day after day, it will get easier, and things will change. Cross my heart.

When you go through this book, highlight the ideas most in line with your vision and your temperament as well as the ones that warm you for no particular reason. Then, *do the work*.

Your Ex May Not Support Your Change

Like a classic 4-year-old tantrum thrower, he may even escalate, becoming more inappropriate and outrageous to recapture the rush he's used to getting from tormenting you—anything to shake you out of your "Lord's Prayer" trance. He knows there's a little window for him to rush in there and blow your mind again before you become a surefooted goddess.

You're going to change so life as he knows it is going to change too.

But he'll get used to it, so hold on and keep at it.

Affirmations

1. Every day, in every way I'm making my life better and better.
2. I am willing to follow through with my commitments.
3. I am ready to come face-to-face with my dreams.

4. LEAN TOWARD EASY

Why spend time devising Mensa-level schemes, when something you saw on a Saturday-morning cartoon would work just as well, or something your 5-year-old said, or the slip from last night's fortune cookie? Remember that my fondest source of inspiration that first year was *Muppet Baby* movies.

Let me give you some examples of how you can simplify your "ex" issues:

Twenty-six-year-old Lisa's ex-husband of three years typically tracked foul-smelling dirt through her house when he came to pick up their 2-year-old son, David, for the weekend. So foul, in fact, she once told me, without cracking a smile, that she suspected he purposely drove out to a farm and jumped around in manure before he came to get David. Frustrated, she began dropping David off at her ex's place, even though it was inconvenient for her and often left her racing to a Friday-night exercise class.

Hello. Simplicity would have told her to ask her ex to wait at the door or take his shoes off and leave them outside.

Forty-year-old Terese's 6-year-old twins left expensive toys she bought at their father's. She reminded them for at least an hour before they left to bring the toys home and followed up with a footnote to her ex as he shuffled them out the door. After all of her nagging, some of the toys never made it back. Imagine that? Terese, fired up over having her instructions dismissed, often swung by her ex's the next day for a showdown, or punished the children.

Simplicity would have said leave the toys wherever they ended up. What difference did it make where the rag doll, a few windup thingamabobs, and some plastic Legos crashed?

Work on putting easy first by waking up your intuition. You know, the little voice that says, "Go right" when you're in a strange city and that right leads you back to your hotel, and predicts the name of a caller before the phone even rings. It has things to tell you now if you'll just listen.

Now, use all of your senses to summon up a familiar bad scene with your ex you'd like to experience differently. Feel the feelings of being in that event. What do you see, hear, and sense? Really put yourself in the picture, and then ask, *"How can I change the outcome?"*

A solution *will* come. Maybe in Surround Sound. Maybe in a half-whisper. Maybe instantly. Maybe days later. But, as long as it's not unhealthy, illegal, or immoral, try it the next time your ex gives you the opportunity.

Forty-eight-year-old Lynn, permanently separated from her lover of 20 years, shared the following story: "For almost a year the kids' father paid child support each month in wads of smoky $5 and $10 bills, with an occasional bad word scribbled on a bill. I kept asking for checks and giving him deposit slips because who wants $500 in small, smelly bills. Then, one morning, as I was driving to work, the light went on and I wondered what he would do if I started thanking him for the small bills by saying it made allowances, lunch, and movie money easier to dole out to our two teens. I tried it, and he was so surprised I didn't grumble or wince that he couldn't even get a sincere 'you're welcome' out. He began writing checks shortly thereafter."

Once you've devised your working mix—5 to 10 simple strategies you can use to quickly defuse acute "situations" and systematically dismantle chronic conniptions—run them through this test:

1. Can you sum it up in a sentence or less?
2. Can you do it immediately, with few props?
3. Does it work?

Affirmations

1. I enjoy simplifying my life.
2. I adore the way things flow when I keep my life light.

5. BE YOUR OWN FAIRY GODMOTHER

Do you suppose Cinderella would have ever gotten to the ball without her fairy godmother, or do you think she had a backup plan? When I read her story to a couple of my little friends at a party one evening, after making a note to trash the book, I asked them how she could have gotten a fancy dress and a ride to the ball without fairy godmom. And the roundtable went something like this:

Kensie, 6, who had an older sister: She could have secretly "borrowed" one of her stepsisters' dresses. They had so many they wouldn't have noticed.

Anne, 7: Yeah, they were kind of chunky though. Did Cinderella know how to sew? She could have cut up one of their dresses and made two.

Jerry, 7, who really wanted to watch a karate movie instead of listen to stories: She looks fine to me, except she just needs to wash her face and comb her hair. Singers on MTV wear stuff like that all the time.

Anne: My mom gets clothes for us from the church sometimes or the secondhand stores. Did they have places like that back in that day?

Jerry: Once my mom bought a dress for a Christmas dance and then she took it back two days later and got her money back.

Kensie: Could she have walked to the ball, or caught the bus or subway with an all-day pass? What about a van-pool?

Jerry: Why did she want to go to the ball anyway? If her stepmom and stepsisters were going, maybe she could finally get some sleep.

Magical minds come in all ages, so I just know that you came up with a few other options for Cindy too.

Please don't ever wait for someone to tap you with a wand and bring your dreams to life. Use the creativity that abounds in you to reshape your own life.

Think-athons

Whenever I feel hopelessly brain-dead over something that's going wrong in my life, I invert my body for about 15 minutes with a shoulder stand to get the blood back to my brain, or let my head dangle off my bed, or put my legs up the wall. Then I get a pad of legal paper and write down all the ways out of the drama—from sensible to outlawed in 38 states.

Starting with a few ideas that often begin with "cry," "pray," and "scream," I sit there—sometimes for hours—until I run out of thinks. When it's all over, somewhere in my scribblings, I have something that will get me moving through my life again.

The next time you get stuck, you can create your own think-along book to scoot yourself forward too. Here's an example:

Situation: My ex badmouths me to our friends.
Possibilities:

Scream.	Pray.	Blow it off.
Tell him to stop.	Pay him to stop.	Ask his mother to make him stop.

Tell friends not to repeat any of his badmouthing.	*Get new friends he doesn't know.*	Teach the dog to drool on him.
Develop selective hearing.	Sue him for slander.	Pamper myself more.
Thank him for the insults.	Have myself hypnotized so it will no longer bother me.	*Laugh.*

Questions

Have you ever noticed that when someone else asks you a question, you try to come up with an answer? Get in the habit of interrogating yourself with some of these questions when you need ideas:

1. What shall I do next?
2. What can I do to move through this?
3. How can I comfort myself in a healthy way?
4. Is there something else I need to know about this situation?
5. Who can help?

Don't worry if you don't get a five-second solution. Difficult things come and go. So do the pearls. Be gentle with yourself and cultivate your creativity. Something will reveal itself at just the right moment.

Arts and Crafts

One of the things I loved most about my ex was that he owned more craft supplies than I did. Together, we were a holiday bazaar waiting to happen. He is a gifted artist, and

I, according to those who know me best, am apparently unable to dress myself or wrap a gift without creative drama.

That same inventive, anything's-possible-if-I've-got-enough-glue spirit that flows through me when I make jewelry, candles, covered boxes, journals, paper, envelopes, and aromatherapy products often spills over into the more left-brained things I have to do in life, and it often comes in handy when I have to dance with Pooh-bah.

As you create, you will become more creative too. Your problem-solving skills will expand as you become more accustomed to weaving a little bit of this-and-that into a work of art.

Arts and crafts are also relaxing. Usually, I do a project a week for the pure joy of it, but when I'm working through something with Pooh-bah, or anyone for that matter, I go into production like one of Santa's toy-shop elves. One weekend last year I made 100 candles. Fifty of them were for a holiday bazaar. The other 50 kept me from committing Pooh-bahcide. I gave most of them away for the holidays, and, well, a girl can never have enough candles so I kept some. I'm on my last five now. Do you have any artsy-craftsy hobbies? Break them out or get some and decorate your life, solve your problems, and relax.

Keep creating.

Affirmations

1. Within me, I have all of the solutions to my challenges.
2. I am always flowing with new ways to make my life more wondrous.
3. I enjoy being creative.
4. I am open to new ideas and experiences.

6. SHOWER YOURSELF WITH TLC

If things in your life are not the way you'd like them to be, it's time for a lot of TLC. Why not comfort yourself in ways that will either help you manifest your heart's desire or live with the reality of not having it? Lower your hysteria level, brush off those ex cooties, and bring yourself back to life with 12 of my favorite comfort rituals:

Altar Time

Most of the time, I feel like I live inside an altar. Candles everywhere. Incense burning. Hypnotic objects and pictures hanging on the walls.

The grand kahuna—my bedroom altar—sits at the foot of my bed. It is nested on a piece of purple velvet sprinkled with candles, gemstones, prayer notes, assorted trinkets from my travels that look like they cost 99 cents, a bouquet of flowers, and a hand-carved purple-heart pen. Above it hangs a breathtaking portrait of a ballet dancer cast against the night sky.

And there I sit in front of this tabletop replica of my innermost desires, of what I consider holy, every night to center, pray, and reminisce. It whispers back, "Be still, be quiet, reflect, and keep dreaming."

On particularly scary days, I've been known to retreat to my bed for an hour or so with Reiki and a Yanni CD to watch my altar candles burn until the sacredness of life returns to me.

If you don't have an altar, I want you to create one before you move on to the next section. Simple is fine. So is having a living altar that changes to meet your needs. Set it up in a private place, like your bedroom. If your children are small, keep it high—on top of a dresser—and instruct them (and visitors) not to touch.

Prayer

For the first 20 years of my life, I barely believed in God, and I prayed only as a last resort, never really expecting it to work because, after all, I was just talking to myself.

I was prolific with tacky preludes like "What is this about?" and "Didn't you hear me yesterday?" and fillers that involved deal-cutting, ultimatums, time lines, demands for preferential treatment, and threats of becoming a full-fledged atheist if I didn't get exactly what I wanted.

I only know that God works in mysterious ways, because to this day I cannot put my finger on when the shift occurred. Now, praying is often the equivalent of being shot with a tranquilizer gun, minus the sting. I don't always get what I ask for, but the consolation is free anesthesia and peace of mind.

I have no real proof of God, but I would rather believe there's somebody watching over me and mine than not. Chris, a 29-year-old divorcée, says, "I've never been much of a churchgoer, and I still wouldn't call myself a *religious* person at all, but I do believe in God, and I've found prayer to be so relaxing and sustaining since my divorce. Sometimes my mother suggests a Bible passage; sometimes I fumble through and find one of my own. Sometimes I stick requests in my Bible. The time I spend praying every day makes my life right again."

As scripts go, there are no right or wrong words—except for the ones I used to use. On your knees, lying down, walking, dancing, bicycling, singing, your task is simply to commune with God, in your own special way, and then hold the faith. Because God is God, She already knows what you think you want or need, so prayer is a redundant comfort ritual. A bullet to chew on while the life surgery takes place. Some days, I imagine God up there with one hand on hip, the other on cloud, saying something like, "Oh no, she didn't just ask me to zap her ex into Kermit the Frog again."

If you find yourself called to prayer, you will develop a personal style of your own, but here are a few places to begin:

1. Humbly ask for what you want, because when God intercedes in your life it is really a big-time favor. If you don't know what to ask for or you are willing to be led, then pray for spiritual clarity, or pray to be delivered to something much fuller or richer.
2. Throw in a few creative, open-ended options. I like tacking on "Or whatever you think is best" and "I'm in trouble here. You know what to do."
3. Don't hover around a prayer request like a hungry, neurotic vulture. Cast it and then march on, doing what you can to be able to say "never mind" at your next prayer session.
4. Close with "Thank you." It's just good manners.
5. Never, ever suggest that God has a hearing problem. Pay close attention to how your life unfolds. You may not always get what you want, but you will get what you need.
6. "Help!" is a complete sentence and prayer.

In *The Handbook of Positive Prayer,* Hypatia Hasbrook also recommends prayer letters. Write a letter to God asking for what you want, read it aloud, and then place it in your Bible or holy book near a passage that is appropriate for the concern, or on your altar. Read the letter every night for three weeks, and then give thanks and burn it whether good has appeared or not.

Meditation

I went to an introductory meditation workshop for the first time during my junior year of college expecting levitation and life-altering insights. When that didn't happen in the first five minutes, I got terribly bored with the inside of my eyelids, the woo-woo flute music, and the incense that smelled faintly illegal. My butt hurt and I wanted to giggle because the person next to me had started to grunt.

In no time at all, I drifted back to the circle of worries that had brought me to the workshop in the first place: the calculus test the next morning and the winning lotto numbers that would pay for my second semester.

The instructor must have remembered his own first meditation experience. He knew we were drifting. Every 10 minutes or so, he would say "Breathe" and "Be here now" and "Pay attention to your breath" and "Enjoy being still." Because of his gentle nagging, I managed to sit there long enough to renew myself.

Over the years, meditation has continued to be an incredible source of nourishment. That first experience is still my foundation, but these days I prefer 10 to 15 minutes to 60, supplemented with meditative streams that happen in the middle of life-on-the-run.

I'm going to share two simple techniques that work well for me, but I encourage you to explore other methods for the next few months too. The best practice is the one that comforts you, sedates you, and whispers "sanctuary." When you find it, do it every day and after a while you will find your life is a moving meditation.

If you are new to meditation, you might have an easier

time gliding into your sessions if you do a few relaxing stretches first or start after a warm bath. Dabbing a tissue with lavender essential oil and holding it over your face for a few minutes before you begin or lighting some incense will also help settle you down. Feel your way into it, and be patient.

Breathing Meditation

Sit or kneel in front of your altar in an erect, dignified posture, with your spine straight. If it's up high, sit in a chair.

Close your eyes, and put one hand on your abdomen. Isolate your breath by deliberately exaggerating your inhalations and exhalations for a few moments. When you inhale, let your abdomen rise and then allow it to completely collapse on your exhale. Once you're familiar with the rhythm of this full breath, normalize it so that it is still deep but no longer labored, and then let your hand drop to your lap, letting both of them now rest with your palms upward. If you feel tension in any area of your body, direct your breath to this area and breathe into it for a few breaths.

Return to your breath if you get distracted by thought parades, and silently repeat one of these affirmations:

"My thoughts are still."

"I am completely relaxed and present."

Do this twice a day for 10 to 15 minutes, preferably when you rise and again before you retire. You can even combine it with counting your blessings.

Candle Meditation

Retreat to your altar, darken the room, and light a candle. Position yourself so that you are seated comfortably in front of the lit candle. Inhale and exhale fully several times and then gaze softly at the flame, blinking and breathing naturally.

Quiet your mind with each breath and let your thoughts float into the flickering yellow flame until it is the only thing on your mind. Do this for about 10 minutes. By the way, this is also a great bathtub meditation.

More Pretending

In order to step up your studies in pretending, you'll need to get to know Pollyanna. I mean *really* know her for yourself, beyond the snide remarks cynics have passed on to you. So go get the book and read it twice . . . slowly . . . as if you are 7 years old.

Polly had heart. She was a re-interpretational artist who could take a moldy piece of bread and hype it up like it was a sultan's feast, and I have learned a lot about pretending from her.

Wild, crazy sirens used to go off in my head whenever Pooh-bah picked Esprit up late, late, late, or didn't show or call either. The first time he was over two hours behind—no call, no nothing—I thought he was dead and was trying to figure out how I would break the news to Esprit.

After the seventh time, I resorted to "tardy" reports and requested advance "late notice." Nothing changed. Finally, I shifted into Polly mode on late days and played my favorite pretend game. Here's the story line if it was raining, which it almost always is here in Washington:

He was drenched in a surprise rainstorm at the bus stop (he doesn't drive). He went back home to change clothes. But he didn't have any clean pants, so he had to do laundry. He didn't have detergent, so he had to go to the store. His phone was cut off earlier in the day because he forgot to pay his bill, so he couldn't call.

Come up with Pollyanna scenarios of your own to explain why your ex is being uncooperative, and use them whenever you need to.

Heroes Scrapbook

I've been collecting articles about inspirational people for years and pasting them in my heroes scrapbook. When I turn the pages, I seem to remember that I am not the only one who's had a rocky road, and that often, in comparison, my life has been a lot like a Hawaiian vacation. Most of the snippets are about ordinary people with mental, physical, and economic challenges who have sparkled *anyway*.

Clip pictures and articles of people you admire—everyday people, national figures, it doesn't matter, triumph is triumph—and put together a heroes scrapbook of your own. If you don't find the pictures and articles of people you want, write little briefs about them and stick them into your book. Anyone on the high road is a hero, so give yourself a page too.

Counting Blessings

Once I attended a prosperity workshop, and after introductions, our facilitator asked us to turn to the person next to us and fire off nonstop for several minutes all the things we were thankful for.

I started with the big thanks. My life. Esprit. My family and friends. My good health. My car. Food. But as I went on, I found myself tacking on the color purple, pear apples, waterfalls, sunsets, voice mail, starlit nights, bubble gum, lipstick, and so on. By the time I was done, I wondered why I had even signed up for the workshop since I was oozing prosperity.

I don't have an oil baron's bank account, but I do have a rich, delicious, interesting life, and this simple ritual often reminds me of that. Count your blessings each day for a few minutes and linger in gratitude for the things you do have.

And if for some reason the battle has taken you so far away that you think you don't have anything to be thankful for, then be glad things aren't any worse.

Journeying

You may feel that your ex is well beyond anything you should have to deal with in a lifetime, but who said you had to take all of his monkey gibberish to heart? I have not heard half of the stuff Pooh-bah has said to me . . . because, sometimes, I have been in Disneyland.

I started *journeying* early on in our post-divorce conversations whenever he was argumentative, overheated, elusive or spewing out loaded remarks that had no Earthly connection to our parenting responsibilities. As he was acting up I'd look down at my amethyst thumb ring and put myself into a light trance. Then I took a trip to Toon Town, rode a few rides, got all hugged up by Bugs Bunny and Porky Pig, and reluctantly made my way back to have another go at a positive, civil two-way chit-chat.

You can wander off too when you need time for repose or want to have some fun in a bleak situation.

The first thing to do is find a spot on his shirt, or on the wall behind him, or if you're really good at looking in his eyes without him knowing you're not listening to a word he's saying, look longingly into his eyes. Meanwhile, as you're looking at the spot on the wall, or his shirt, or into his eyes, imagine you're on your last vacation, or your next vacation, or mentally make out your grocery list, or pick out lottery numbers. Zoom in on any scene that pleases you and stay there until you imagine he's almost done, or you see his brows rising in the annoyed way they would if he thought you weren't listening to him.

If you journey on the phone, a mute button is a must. Hum along if you want until he pauses, or carry on your own little diatribe until it's time for you to reply. Test your mute button the next time he calls by depressing it and asking him a question he'd be likely to respond quickly to: "I've got two tickets for Hawaii. I'm not going to be able to go after all, and I can't refund them. Would you like them?"

If he answers, say "Just kidding" and get a new phone with a working mute button; if not, play, play, play.

Witnessing

Witnessing is a detachment tool, similar to journeying, that allows you to intricately survey a troubling event without going to pieces.

It is simple enough to practice the next time your child is doing something you don't particularly like, for example, leaving a trail of suds from the bathroom to her room. Witnessing happens in your head, so if you want to, encapsulate your thoughts in cartoon bubbles.

What you do is think something like "Oh look, Esprit is making a suds trail from the bathroom to her room." Describe the suds. Feel yourself getting worked up. "Man, look at those huge blobs of suds she's making! Haven't I told her to dry herself off before she leaves the bathroom a zillion times? My head hurts, my stomach is tight. Okay, she's in her room now."

Don't do anything. Don't say anything. Just quietly follow this internal dialogue and keep watching your child and noting what you see and feel. Then if you have to do something or say something to clean up a mess, do or say it calmly.

Witness your ex.

Say he is standing two feet in front of you, yelling at you. Your inner witness chatter might go something like this:

"So, he's calling me stupid, lazy, and fat. Those words all end with consonants. Wow, look at how big his eyes are getting. His eyebrows are moving together like a unibrow. I wonder how many cavities he's had . . . and look he's still got his tonsils. I want to stuff a live grenade in there. He's such a turd. Would I give him mouth-to-mouth if he passed out from this fit? I'm going to scream. Okay, he's winding down. Let me close and get out of here."

So What?

"So what?" is one of my favorite mantras because it often nips many a real or manufactured assault in the bud and helps me lighten up. I use it at least 100 times a day to prevent high blood pressure, heart attacks, headaches, deranged vindictive behavior, and general day-to-day human weirdness and stress. Try it out for yourself on some of the dingers below:

- Your son informs you that your ex carries a picture of you in his wallet so he can badmouth you wherever he goes.
- Your ex tells you your new couch sucks.
- Your ex laughingly points out a pimple on your chin.
- Your daughter says your ex calls you "monkey-girl" to his wife.

Don't hang on Pooh-bah's every insult. Blow it off, lighten up, and "so what?" yourself back to a positive frame of mind.

Smiling

Smiling can rapidly shift your mood. Start first thing in the morning by greeting yourself in the mirror with a genuine smile and a "Good morning, goddess/angel/princess/sweetie" (whatever it is you think you'd like to hear every morning). It also helps a lot if you start the day in silk pj's.

Place a small mirror in your purse or wallet and repeat this greeting to your reflection at least 10 times a day. You can do it in your car, you can do it in a store window, or you can say it to your reflection in someone else's glasses. You can smile into a puddle or a blank computer screen, a window, holiday ornaments, water, silverware. Are you getting this?

Pamper, Pamper, Pamper

Nothing is quite so awful when you have silk pj's, the right shade of lipstick, and a teddy bear.

Seven years ago, I would have no more spent 15 minutes polishing my nails or soaking in a bubble bath than I would have had my tongue pierced. Believe it or not, Esprit was my first pampering role model. As I watched her pile every soft, silky fabric and fluffy stuffed animal onto her bed to rest with as a toddler, I couldn't help but think that the child was under the impression she'd gotten dropped off at the palace.

And it really is a hypnotic affair to watch the teenage iteration prop herself up against me by the fireplace, fluff pillows under her knees, and artfully French-tip her nails and apply lotion to her hands. You'd think at any moment some handmaiden were going to sashay over to her with some lemonade, massage her feet, and fan her, but usually it's just me.

I hope she stays this way.

Esprit passed on many of her favorite pampering rituals to her recovering tomboy mother. She started me off with nail polishing. I hadn't planned on liking anything that required my hands to be indisposed for half an hour, but she was so excited that I was even considering it that I gave in. File, buff, base coat, polish. By the time we got to topcoat I was sprung. Decadence in a bottle, and then onto my nails.

I began stocking up on nail polish, bubble bath, body oils, silk pj's, lipsticks with names like Passionate Plum and Purple Sunset, and running through them like I was Cleopatra to the third power.

I discovered body glitter and body dust, vanilla-scented baths, and mango cream. Now, I cannot imagine life any other way.

Pamper yourself because you can. Do it because it feels delicious. Do it because pampering is a powerful painkiller. You deserve to have overwhelming evidence of pleasure in your life, and if it comes from nowhere else, it should come from you to you.

Before you become the pampering priestess, you should make sure you're taking care of your body's basic needs. Visit your doctor for a complete "wellness" exam. Ask about incorporating whole, healthy, living foods into your diet. At the very least, drink lots of clean water and stop eating artificially colored products that contain ingredients that end with "ugar," "eine," "ate," and "ite."

Your next stop is the gym or fitness center. Ask one of the trainers to create an exercise routine for you, or follow someone around who looks the way you want to look and ask her what she does. Even if you're as skinny as Olive Oyl, regular workouts reduce anxiety, uplift the spirits, increase stamina, and keep the temple toned.

Next, make a master pampering list of healthy, positive, uplifting things that deeply please you. Then, even if you think the list is simple enough to remember, copy it onto an index card, have it laminated, and stick it in your purse or wallet. They don't have to be expensive, or even take you away from home. If you haven't taken much time for pampering and you're not sure what pleases you, ask yourself the following question in the mirror once a day for a week: "What can I do to please you?"

Whatever it is, whatever you like, as long as it's healthy, do it—in good times and in bad.

Once you finish your list, get your day planner out and schedule pampering sessions with yourself every day for the next month. If you don't have a planner, do it on a plain piece of paper or stick 30 notes on the refrigerator—whatever will work best in your head. *Please do this. It will feed your soul and keep the goddess happy.*

CLEOPATRA BATH

What you will need:
   One 4-lb. box of epsom salts
   One 16-oz. box of baking soda
   4 tablespoons of lavender essential oil*
   10 drops of lemon essential oil*
Optional:
   1 cup of Dead Sea salts
   7 drops of food coloring

Stir together in a large bowl until well mixed and store the mixture in mason jars, canisters, or plastic baggies. Pour ½ cup to 1 cup under running tub faucet.

   *Lavender oil melts away tension and lemon oil lifts the spirits. You can find them both in most health stores.

A Day Without Words

Often as part of my pampering quota for the month, I spend a day in silence. Without words, I can finally listen clearly to my own inner dialogue, and view my thoughts, beliefs, and the words I might have spoken in a very unencumbered way.

Without words, I can often develop the stillness and wisdom to purge toxic thoughts from my mind, the way a body fast flushes toxins from my body. Without words, I quickly discover what it is I really want to give voice to.

Here's how you can plan your own Day Without Words retreat at home:

1. Arrange to have someone watch your children for a day (if they won't be spending time with their dad).
2. Tell your family and friends beforehand that you will be unavailable for the day.
3. Unplug the phone, radio, and TV.
4. Stay inside, and don't answer the door.
5. Do your chores around home, pamper yourself, meditate, read, eat, dance around the house, whatever you want, but don't say anything for the entire day.

Enjoy.

Affirmations

1. It's okay to put my own well-being first.
2. I enjoy treating myself well, and I will take time to do it.
3. I adore myself and I deserve to be pampered.
4. Every day, I celebrate my life and I love who I am.
5. I take time each day to spiritually center and renew myself.

7. Learn to Playact

*"A strong man masters others.
A truly wise man masters himself."*
—The Wisdom of the Taoists

Half the battle in interacting with a challenging ex is keeping your composure, on good days and bad, until your child is grown and gone.

Sometimes you will be able to whirl and twirl your way into an authentic display of good home training, but sometimes it's going to have to be a big, fat, hairy, Academy Award–winning, somebody-get-me-an-Oscar! performance.

It doesn't matter how you get there, just get there.

When you are upset:

- *Your* blood pressure increases.
- *You're* more accident prone. I wonder how many women rear-end another car thinking about some crappy thing their ex said to them the night before.
- *You're* more likely to displace your negative feelings toward the innocents. Do your kids end up with some of the fallout of a bad-ex day?
- Stress zaps *your* energy, creativity, and joy. How much time do you want to spend getting over every other conversation with your ex?
- *You* tend to look slightly unattractive because your face is all scrunched up.

Did you notice all the yucky things happen to *you*?

Playacting

When I suggested playacting, a second cousin to pretending, to 32-year-old Wanda, who often ends up self-medicating her after-ex headaches with Rocky Road ice cream and Chardonnay, she told me it sounded manipulative. I told her to think of it as a cheap, low-fat headache remedy. When she resisted, I asked her to tell me what she thought might work better, and she suggested the following line:

"You're being selfish, immature, unreasonable, spiteful, and mean."

I asked if she would be willing to try that phrase for a month, and she told me she'd used it . . . at least once a week . . . for the past three years. Does this seem like a flawed example of personal growth, or is it just me?

I bet you a quarter these words won't bring on an Ex Charming epiphany in your Pooh-bah either. They certainly didn't work on Wanda's ex. He thought she was patronizing him and escalated. More headaches, more Rocky Road, and more Chardonnay followed.

Playacting, on the other hand, can help you remain calm, confident, scripted, and powerful. Picture this visitation pickup scenario:

Your ex drives up 30 minutes late to pick up the children, honks the horn impatiently for several minutes, and then comes to the door and knocks—BAM! BAM! BAM!—as if you had your hearing aid turned down low.

When he steps inside, he says your window plant looks dead, and what is that smell coming out of the kitchen (your dinner), and why can't you ever have the children completely ready when he comes?

You could open the door in a huff, say something about him being a day late and a dollar short, the horn and all, or you could open the door with a smile and a hello. "Won't you sit down? Tea? . . . I'll see if the children are ready."

In playact mode, you keep it short and polite. "More tea? Do you want to see some new pictures of the kids? . . . Oh, look, here they come. Kids, have fun with your father. See you Sunday. Bye-bye."

Thirty-something Carla was used to her ex-husband Rod barking orders when he came to pick up their 7- and 9-year-olds. "Get John's other shoes and put them in the bag. This bag is too big anyway, go get a smaller one. Speaking of small, did you have breast reduction surgery or do they just look shrunken because they're sagging?"

Carla's customary reflex response was a penetrating, blow-for-blow sarcastic throttle. But she was tired of the animosity, tired of the tension, tired of being hoarse the next day, just plain tired, so she went cold turkey on her 7-year-old's birthday. "When my ex came by to drop off his birthday gift and tried to bulldoze me, I passed him a party favor with my best Julia Roberts grin painted on, and thanked him for being such a loving father. Then, while his jaw was still hanging on the carpet, I turned, said I was going to bring the cake out, and asked if he would light the candles. He smiled his first real smile in two years that day over the cake, and he's relaxed his assaults a lot since then."

Many moons ago, master motivational coach Tony Robbins used to tuck me in at night with bedtime stories of how changing my breathing, body language, and the pitch and cadence of my voice when I was having a demoralizing moment would help me quickly shift from pitiful to powerful. As I listened to his taped *Personal Power* series for months on continuous play, I became better and better at impersonating my goddess self even when I didn't feel like it.

In a moment, I'm going to share a few of those basics with you to use when playacting with your ex, but first I want you to close your eyes right now and take a few moments to recall your most recent challenging moment with him. Choose a time when you were feeling a little out of control, put off, or powerless, and walk through it, recounting your body language in Memorex detail. Then open your eyes and describe it in the margin. Did your eyes flinch or water? Head drop? Jaws tighten? Face frown? Shoulders knot up or slump down? Head throb? Breath quicken?

Now, I want you to go back in and tinker with that same scene. Pretend you were feeling calm and composed, and run through the event again. What's happening? Where's your head? What's the expression on your face? How's your breathing?

Make your body over this way, or use the 30-second shift below and playact your little heart out the next time your ex acts up.

The 30-Second Shift

Take a few deep inhalations and exhalations. Keep your head level, but consciously relax your forehead, eyes, and jaws. You might even let your lips part slightly. If your shoulders are raised, let them drop, but not to the level where it looks like you're getting ready to cry. Breathe in and out, deeply, but with a gentle rhythm. Stand up straight and scan your body for tension, and lovingly tell any tight spots to relax. Then plant a glowing, I-love-myself-and-this-is-easy smile on your face.

Midori, a self-described hot-blooded 37-year-old who was a common-law spouse for almost a decade, said it made her skin itch to paste on the happy face and be cheery toward her ex at first. "How was I supposed to smile at someone who'd just said he didn't know why he had had children with me in the first place? But after a few months of thinking about it, I figured, what the heck? It might make our daughter's life simpler. So I put it on. I smiled. I was polite. He was less of a butt, our daughter was happy, and when he left, I took a bubble bath and blasted Barry Manilow until I was happy too."

It may be awkward, but do it. It will grow on you, and it will eventually help you become genuinely mellower around your ex.

The Spock Technique

Spock, a very mild-mannered Vulcan character on the original *Star Trek*, was one of my early anger management mentors when I was a teenager. Like most Vulcans, Spock was taught to suppress his feelings from a young age, so he was about as reactive as an ATM machine.

There were quite a few times when his eyes should have been popping out of his head—like when the ship was on fire, or the crew was being pursued by evil scale-faced aliens—but Mr. ATM never blinked.

Here's how you can imitate him.

1. Stay focused on your objective.
2. Speak in a monotone voice. Listen to the instructional message on your voice mail (the voice that tells you what to do to check your messages). Take a little cheeriness out of it if your lady is upbeat. Mine isn't. If you don't have voice mail, call the "time" or "weather" number, and rehearse that inflection. Matter-of-fact, succinct, and dry is your goal.
3. Lob back troubling comments with thoughtful, logical, calm responses.
4. Install a dial-tone look on your face if he continues to rant.

Immediately following a Spock skit, go dancing or running, or do something that makes your heart race. This will keep you from permanently becoming Ms. ATM machine.

COMPOSURE PRACTICE

Make a list of the things that your ex does that normally turn your stomach—perhaps the list you used in *High Road Jeopardy!* Give a copy to your friends, and coach them with your ex's standard scripts, tonality, gestures, and comebacks. Then have them play the role of your ex so you can practice using playacting or the Spock technique.

Use playacting and the Spock technique often as emergency intervention tools to help you conjure up a temporary powerful altered state when under duress.

Affirmations

1. I am learning to cherish my ability to control my internal states.
2. I can be calm and relaxed anytime I want to.
3. I decide how I will behave in the world.

8. Keep Things in Perspective

Perspective is subtracting the scummy things from the splendor and deciding you have enough to carry on. It is also subtracting the things you can't stand about your ex from the things you used to love, and the things you would like about him if he were anybody else in the world who hadn't given you so much grief, and advancing him the benefit of the difference.

There are endless ways to describe life with your Poohbah. One day, my separated 40-ish coworker Marge told me she had heard a Halloween movie commercial that perfectly described her ex. "One hundred thirteen of the damned have just escaped from hell, and they're headed your way." Because I also knew her ex, who in some ways was borderline sinister toward her, there was no denying his sins. Then again, I also knew how gentle and generous he was with his 13- and 16-year-old daughters. I knew—divorced or otherwise—he was one of the few men who took the time to learn their friends' names, to send them just-because-I-was-thinking-of-you notes, and to take sick hours from his job many Fridays to pick them up early after school. Yes, he called Marge "Miss Piggy" now and then, and meant it. Yes, he had had several affairs during their 17-year marriage, but all in all, he was not the through-and-through demented maniac she made him out to be.

There's usually a strand of decency in everyone, even knotheads. So find something to like him for. What is he doing right? Is he great with the kids, financially supportive, has he ever made any household repairs for you? What does he *not* do that you're grateful for? Has he ever not called you Miss Piggy, or jotted your name and phone number on the stall door in the guys' bathroom at the local bar with a suggestion that you might be a little wild and kinky? While you're keeping Pooh-bah's pluses in perspective, being a glass-half-full goddess, roll the positive aspects of your other relationships, family life, career, and spirituality to the front of your brain too, and celebrate them. A hundred times a day is not nearly enough, but start there.

What it comes down to is deciding how you are going to describe your life. Are you going to tell your tale from the perspective of someone who's been beaten down 5,000 times and is scared to hold her head up again? Or from the throne, in goddess-ese, which goes something like this, "Yeah girl, parts of that ex thing were hell, but I'm over it now, and my life is sweet."

Affirmations

1. Something is always right in my life.
2. I am willing to thoroughly acknowledge all of my wins.
3. I choose to repair my life with loving hands.
4. My perspective determines my experience.

9. Reduce Your Ex Cooties

Have you ever noticed that sometimes you know shortly after meeting someone who's having trouble with their ex that they're having trouble with their ex?

Once in a Thai cooking class, we went around the room introducing ourselves and one of my classmates blurted out, "I'm Sandi. I have two children who like Thai food. I've been divorced from their dad for three years, and I've got full custody because he's a punk."

Shortly after my divorce, I got a new coworker who told me much more about her ex—whom she referred to as Attila—than I ever wanted to know. She ran through his transgressions with fresh, thick grief throughout the day. We were two weeks into her true confessions before she revealed that they'd been divorced for 10 years, her son was 23, and she was remarried.

There is not one woman with a Pooh-bah who will not have the temptation to do the occasional "smearcast" now and then. (If you find one, check her pulse.) Sometimes life with Pooh-bah hurts, and that hurt can preempt ordinary moments when you're supposed to be learning to cook Pad Thai or talking over a new project with a coworker. But the more you swirl the gunk round and round in your mind and over your tongue, the more you keep it alive, and the crazier you become. Forgetting and forgiving will help protect your mental health, and it is your path to freedom.

Forgetting

In most spiritual growth models, forgiving precedes for-getting, but I've found it easier if you flip them around. If you forget as many of your ex files as you can first, there will be less to forgive.

If you're shaking your head right now, thinking there's no way you're going to let me talk you into letting him off the hook for any of the foul stuff he's done, I'm with you, but answer me this: Is clinging to them contributing to your well-being and growth? Hmmmmmmm? Don't pretend your answer was "yes" either.

When I posed this question to one of my NGAWYEM callers, the way she resisted, you would have thought I'd asked her to fork over a kidney. Her ex had left her for her cousin, and he kept telling the children she was keeping them from him, even though he was the one who was for-ever flying out of town to tend to company business. Who was I to take away her right to be pissed off at him?

Anger is a reasonable response to betrayal, but we have choices, you and I, about the emotions and thoughts we let lead us. Do you really want squatter's rights on anything that is eating out your insides? Or would you rather discard it and grab hold of some feelings that have a bigger payoff?

Selective Amnesia

Friends always think my memory is a little off when I strain to recall a monumental, sanity-altering Pooh-bah event, an event I no doubt shared with them shortly after the fact. Some of them, I imagine, have even considered having me tested for dementia. I think I would fail the test, but there's no deny-ing that I have clearly slipped into my memory banks and spliced most of my Pooh-bah A.D. archive tapes, because I think I would come as permanently unglued as Humpty-Dumpty if I reeled through his uncut bloopers too often.

Say I have a terrible, terrible moment with him, and I've got my selective amnesia feature turned on—here's what happens:

1. I detach.
2. I delete details I don't like.
3. I generalize.
4. I dilute the experience with positive self-talk or activity.

One time after one of my "tardy" reports, he started yelling and frothing, but when the worst of it passed through my selective amnesia filter, all I had left was:

1. He was mad.
2. He said something bad about me.
3. It was a yucky moment.
4. I went for a bike ride with Esprit.

Generalize and blur your historical impressions of unpleasant times, and then chase them down with a happy. They will be much easier to release.

If you feel you need to hold on to some bad memory for your memoirs, write it down, date it, and get back to your joy. My journals fill in where my selective memory fails. For certain parts of this book, I reread passages from old journals to refresh myself (unfortunately—or fortunately—I recorded the whole damn thing).

Forgiving

Forgiving Pooh-bah doesn't mean you have to flop down at his feet and beg for more torture, relinquish child support, tongue-kiss him again, or agree that the stupid, evil stuff he did was okay. You don't even have to tell him you forgave him.

Forgiving is letting go of your anger, resentment, and disappointment toward another person, and it will allow you to spend more of your life energy on something other than hating Pooh-bah's guts.

I decided to forgive my ex after reading somewhere that forgiveness was the first step in reclaiming personal power. It was an ongoing experiment. And after over 200 attempts, it took.

Healing the R.A.S.H.'s

Pretending does not work with forgiving, and I had to go back and unearth a ton of buried *resentments, anger, sadness,* and *hurt* (R.A.S.H.'s) before the forgiveness thing took. It was excruciating and I napped a lot, but I kept at it.

Toward the end, when most of the digging was done and the haunting relics of our relationship were spread out in front of me, my friend Alma—who I'm sure wishes Pooh-bah would secretly run off and join the circus, but has never said so—gave me an assignment that helped me gather them up and trade them in for something much more valuable. She gave me $50 and told me to spend it on things I wish he had done for me while we were married. Resisting the temptation to be practical and plunk the money down on the light bill, I invested it in my healing.

It took half the day, but when it was over, all of my issues with him were resolved. Maybe because I knew I could do for me what I'd wanted from him, so there was no longer a need to hold on to the R.A.S.H.'s. Maybe because after gathering these things in such a juicy celebration of me, I felt more benevolent. Who cares? It was done.

Here are some of the things I bought/did, and what they symbolized to me.

Cost	Activity/Purchase	Things I Wish He'd Done for Me or with Me
$1	A water bottle and workout	Supported my fitness goals
$2	Fresh carrot juice	Supported my healthy nature
$0	Danced in the rain	Shared my spontaneity
$0	Read an article titled, "Get Ready to Love"	Prepared himself to love me
$7	Wrote special sentiments in blank just-because cards I purchased and bought a mug filled with chocolate kisses that said, "Right now someone who loves you is thinking of you."	Shared random acts of love and thoughtfulness
$2	Plastic red heart filled with M&M's	Loved me with a full heart
$5	Items to make one pair of earrings	Adorned me
$2	Day-Glo purple pen, 10-color pen	Honored the writer me
$5	A mini greenhouse	Planted and nourished more things with me
$6	Surprise grab bag at lingerie store	Noted my love for surprises
$2	*Star Trek* collecting cards	Given me things I liked even if he thought them odd
$6	Lunch at Chinese buffet	Taken me out to eat the foods I love

Cost	Activity/Purchase	Things I Wish He'd Done for Me or with Me
$0	Drove over the bridge at sunset listening to taped love songs	Been romantic
$2	Fire log	Kept me warm

Your Turn

You could do this exercise with $10 or $100. But for now, limit yourself to $50, even if you have more to blow. Less is fine. Some of the things on my list didn't cost a dime. If you have less, clip pictures and words from old magazines to represent things. Money's not the answer here. Symbolism is.

Don't make a list either. Do it in a stream. Your heart will tell you where to go and what to get to heal. I saw Alma at 9:00 that morning and I was finished with everything except the sunset ride by noon. You'll know when you're done.

Place the items that will fit on your altar for at least a week and hang on to this list. We're going to use it again later on in the book.

Flush It

This next exercise will help you remove postdivorce R.A.S.H.'s. But it can also be used monthly or seasonally for further clearing.

Go get a roll of not-so-cushy toilet paper and a fine felt-tip pen. Write down all of your ex's offenses since your breakup. Be brief, and start with the earliest experience you can come up with. Don't stop until you've run out of incidents and do not go back and reread them.

When you've finished, take your wad to the bathroom, light some incense and a candle, and flush away. If you've accumulated a lot of tissue, then break it down into several flushes.

Ready to forgive him now?

If you're not there yet, it's okay. This *is* heart surgery. But put it on your two-year plan. Do it for selfish reasons, do it for God reasons, do it because you don't think he had the skills to behave any other way at the time, do it because I told you to, do it because it will help you head for higher ground.

Affirmations

1. Thank you, God, for all that you have given me,
   For all you have taken away
   And for everything you have left me with.
2. This is a new day and I am excited about its possibilities.
3. I live in the present moment.
4. I look at my life with fresh eyes.

10. Cancel the Pity Party, and Drop That Voodoo Doll

Goddesses don't whine or sulk. And it's not because they don't have reasons to.

I'll make you a deal. If you can name 10 positive things you get out of whining or sulking that at least 10 people who don't have mental problems would agree are delightful, then you have my permission to whine and sulk your heart out. Otherwise, it's time to let go.

Vengeance isn't very useful either, although it can be very invigorating. Very. But it's an animated, childish, short-lived rush. When you are bent on punishing someone by acting dark and small, let me tell you this. *You can never, ever get even. Never.* You will never inflict the same pain, and when you emerge from your wrath, you will look suspiciously like a pitiful, spiny little troll. I know this only because I did a short stint as a pretend voodoo priestess.

One night a little less than six months after my divorce, I arranged some black candles and a picture of my Poohbah on my altar, the way I had seen in some witch movie a long time ago. Then I sat in front of it and pictured him choking on a chicken bone. Not only was I being mean-spirited and macabre, but the time-management junkie me was fit to be tied the next day, because I chucked yoga class to do something that was fundamentally loony-tunes.

I'm proud to report five years of sobriety as a pretend voodoo priestess. Here's a seven-step plan to help you recover from troll-like behaviors:

1. Count your blessings first (see page 41). Maybe your whining, sulking, and other small behaviors aren't warranted.
2. Whine in private. A journal is ideal, but if you are more of an orator, turn on your tape recorder and deliver your woes in front of the mirror. Hopefully, it will be almost impossible to do this for long without cracking up, but if you feel yourself getting whinier and whinier, skip to #4.
3. Never, ever share your troubles with a drama queen or someone who regularly whines to you. She will only take you deeper into the dungeon of your own self-pity, which when unchecked can be rather intoxicating.
4. Give yourself a finite amount of time to snivel. Never exceed 10 minutes.
5. Figure out what positive actions you can take in the future that will reduce your need to repeat this experience.
6. Don't do anything to your ex you would not do to your child. You can think it, but don't talk about it or do it.
7. In general, keep your moaning and groaning to yourself. Don't spend time talking about how your ex did this-or-that or didn't do this-or-that.

Here are a few techniques for constructively releasing anything that might prompt you to backslide into whining, sulking, or plotting revenge.

1. Cancel, Cancel

I learned this wonderful technique when I studied the Silva mind-control method. It's very simple, very quick. Whenever you have a smoldering thought, follow it up with "Cancel, cancel." Do this over and over until your aggravation disappears.

2. Happy Count

Breathing deeply, but naturally, with your eyes closed, count backward from 50, relaxing as you go. When you get to 1, create a picture in your mind of the last time you were completely happy, and allow yourself to linger in this scene for 5 to 10 minutes.

3. Exploding Balloons

Sit or lie down in a quiet spot. Close your eyes and count backward from 10 to 1, breathing in and out deeply as you go. Visualize a balloon of any color. Put your current frustration into the balloon and then let it float off. When you've watched it rise a safe distance from you, pop it and release the frustration to the wind.

Small Thoughts Journal

Buy a journal or notebook today and label it "Small Thoughts Journal." Keep it locked or tucked away until you feel a "moment" coming on. When you do, pull it out, date the page, and fill it with pitiful or vile scribble for 10 minutes, because that's your limit, remember? Play with these starter phrases:

"I'm so sick of . . ."

"I'm really frustrated right now because . . ."

"Woe is me. I . . ."

"I think my ex is a . . ."

"I wish I had a . . . , so I could . . ."

"I cannot believe that dirty . . ."

"I want . . ."

None of this is to say you're not going to lose it here and there. Sonia, who was never a pretend voodoo priestess, says she does have an occasional urge to grab the biggest stick she can find and beat the pulp out of her ex for all the havoc he's caused in her life. She's never done it, but it's one of her favorite Small Thoughts journal exercises. The rest of the time, she's on the high road. Make that your final destination too.

Affirmations

1. I am the keeper of my soul.
2. I no longer have a need to dwell on small things.
3. I can control my behavior by managing my mind.

11. LEAN ON THOSE WHO LOVE YOU

You can sustain yourself for a long time with guts, faith, grace, lipstick, silk pj's, and teddy bear alone, but why not let helping hearts surround you and nurture you now? Whose epitaph ever reads: "And she did it all by herself"? If it does, who's going to be there to read it?

No one makes it all alone, and no one should. And yet, as I interviewed parents for this book, I discovered that most of them were as reluctant to get support as they were to let me use their real names. You may have some of that same resistance, so let's work through two of the biggest reasons they offered for not asking for help, and get them out of your way too.

I'm All Alone

Your nose is growing.

Most of the time, when we are in crisis mode, we withdraw, and that withdrawal often creates the illusion that we are all alone. *But we never are.*

I used to think I was an island—stoic, even if my heart was racing like it was trying to break through some speed barrier. Never asked for help, and if it came unsolicited, I stomped off like someone had told me I had pig breath. Then some people came into my life, and they pretended to be deaf and dumb when I refused their offerings, and they were very, very good at sweet-talking my pride into looking the other way. Again and again they did this, reprogramming me in such a loving, gentle way that while asking for help is still not always the most natural thing in the world, it does always occur as an option when I need it.

You're not an island either. We are all connected. Just as I am connected to you now, and you to me. And we are here to hold each other up. So join the society of people who need people, and make a list of *everyone* you can call on for assistance right now. Family, friends, neighbors, church members, associates, etc. Don't worry about filling in all the blanks. A few good supportive hearts are enough.

As you were putting your list together, did you see people taking on different roles in your recovery? No doubt, you may have some idea of who to call for what, but since we don't always think straight when the sky is falling, jot their general support roles in the margin now.

Meet 24-year-old Brenda's support team:

Person	Call/See For
Mary	Everything, because she knows my heart, she'll listen to me dump, cheer me up, and phone slap me if I need it
John	Laughter, plus he makes great lasagna
Sarah	Quick, meaningful advice, great hugs, and massage
Karen	Money
My pastor	Prayer and words of comfort
My parents	Child care, money, legal advice, loving support
Thomas	Child care, and he's neutral about the kids' dad, so he would be willing to drop them off sometimes

If I Ask for Help I Will Appear Weak

"I need help" are without a doubt three of the most powerful words I know.

Tina, a 46-year-old corporate professional and mother of 7- and 9-year-old girls, says, "It was hard to say to my family and friends, 'My shit is falling apart and I need help,' but it was the thing that saved me. After I said it I almost felt like they had been respectfully hovering in the shadows, watching, silently waiting for my Grand Canyon pride to melt, so I'd ask for help. When it finally did, those loving hands came forward so fast to hold me up and help me put my life back together. My relationships with them deepened, and I felt much more powerful than I would have ever expected, because I asked for what I needed."

I want you to go to the phone after you finish this section and call one of the people on your list and ask for something. I don't care if it's rent money, child care, a good joke, or ice. I don't care. Just ask. Don't do anything else until you make that phone call.

It takes a strong, courageous person to ask for help. The people who love you know this and they will come running to serve you when you call.

Affirmations

1. I draw people into my life who are willing to nurture and support me.
2. I am deeply grateful I have loved ones to watch over me.
3. I am ready to be strong and brave enough to ask for help.

12. Focus, Focus, Focus

If you have the intention to get a handle on your relationship with your ex, you will. And a year from now, or even sooner, you'll be reciting the interview responses on page 22 and having a déjà vu experience.

Since this is life, distractions will probably come along to pull you away from this intention, but like mutant dream-eating buzzards, they must be held at bay, so you can stay on track.

Janet's ex was king buzzard. When they first divorced five years ago after his second affair, he often set 30-year-old Janet off by clucking his teeth at her when she said something he didn't like. Who knows, he might have been trying to piss her off, but it might have been a nervous reaction, or maybe he had a farm-boy fantasy and had chickens on his mind. In any case, she wasted hours afterward seething, whiting out all constructive thoughts of having a peaceful relationship.

To get back to her goddess space, she decided to adopt a rule that if he did annoying things that didn't involve time or money, she'd ignore them, including the clucking.

Patrice, the mother of teenage twins, uses her tick-off meter as a refocusing tool. Whenever her ex tries to ruffle her, she pinpoints the atrocity on the meter. Peanuts is 1, Wage Bloody War is 10. If the meter rises to 8, she breaks out the cannons; otherwise, she passes.

If you're oblivious about how often you bite when you really don't have to, track yourself for a week. Whenever you find yourself upset for longer than a few minutes over "little" ex things, add a tick mark. If at the end of the week you have proof that you were willing to lose your mind over your ex clucking his teeth at you, flip back to the "Me" list you created in chapter 2 and review, review, review.

Affirmations

1. I have choices about how I respond to other people.
2. It is okay to blow off things that do not deserve my attention.
3. Strong intention equals dreams come true.

Ritual #1

Here is a centering ritual you can perform to kick off your high road journey.

What you will need:

- A picture of you, your ex, and your child(ren)
- 2 pictures of you and your child(ren)
- A picture of your ex and your child(ren)
- 3 candles
- 3 index cards or small slips of paper
- A dish to burn notes in

Note: Sketches will do if you don't have pictures.

Place the candles in a triangle shape on your altar, and put the burning dish in the center of the triangle. Lay the picture of your former nuclear family beside the candle at the bottom right point. This candle represents the past.

Lay one of the pictures of you and your children and the picture of your ex and your children at the bottom left point. This candle represents the present.

Lay the other picture of you and your children by the candle at the top of the triangle. This candle represents the future.

Light the candle of the past and write down one reason you're glad you were all once together as a family. Then close your eyes and repeat the following:

I accept everything that has happened between us and I am willing to let go of it and move forward. Bless us all. Thank you.

Place the paper in the dish, light it, and watch it burn.

Next, light the candle of the present and write down something you're grateful for right now. Then close your eyes and repeat the following:

Thank you for giving me this opportunity to begin again. I will do my best to make the most of my situation.

Place the paper in the dish, light it, and watch it burn.

Finally, light the candle of the future and write down one thing you're looking forward to in the future. Then close your eyes and repeat the following:

Lead me to the high road, and I will follow it, as far as I can, for as long as I can, and keep my sense of humor. Thank you.

Place the paper in the dish, light it, and watch it burn.

Sit before your altar for a few minutes in front of the lit candles, and picture pink cords connecting all of the candles. Then, when you're ready, blow out the candles and allow the cords to disintegrate.

❦

It's time for a pampering break. Before you continue, treat yourself to something from your master pampering list.

❦

❧ PART 2 ❧

Communication

"You must do the things you think you cannot do."
—Eleanor Roosevelt

When Pooh-bah told me he hated me and wished I were dead, I thought about hiring an interpreter or surrogate to relay messages, so I'd never have to speak to him again. After a few months of near-cavewoman grunts, sign language, and notes, it was a mystery to me how I would ever get to goddess chat with him when almost everything he said made me want to part his hair with a weed whacker. But I knew in my heart the grunts had to go. The sign language too. So I added a few more intelligent words each time I saw him, and the words became sentences, and I even managed to smile real smiles after a while. Each sentence became a tingling victory for me, because even though he was being Pooh-bah, I was being a goddess, and that had a richness all its own.

13. Release Your Reluctance to Talk to Him

Would you rather not have to chitchat to Pooh-bah because you:

A. Still hate his guts
B. Feel nauseous whenever you hear his voice
C. Think he's evil or dumb
D. Expect another unfruitful conversation that will lead you back to A, B, or C
E. All of the above

And if you could order an Internet-special alien pod-person look-alike to stand in for you when he calls or visits, would you, like me, have a sudden urge to wrap a bunch of streamers around your body and sprint through the neighborhood screaming, "I'm free, I'm free! Thank God almighty, I'm free at last!"

What if I told you that you could achieve that same liberating high by learning how to weave your words and behavior together to create a compelling mind-meld with Pooh-bah? And why would I want to mind-meld with Pooh-bah, you ask? So you can have smart, speedy conversations and get back to painting your toenails.

A successful mind-meld begins with the release of any reluctance and anxiety surrounding your "talk" times, and it ends with strategies and resources for making the mind-meld stick. The next three exercises will prepare you for the first stage. Exercise 1 is designed as a reality check to point out that your life probably is not, and need not be, just one endless conversation with Pooh-bah. Exercise 2 will help you clarify the crummy feelings you associate with talking to him. And Exercise 3 is a visualization to help you do away with those feelings and embrace more useful "talk time" attitudes. You will get the most out of these exercises by doing them sequentially and writing down your answers.

Exercise 1: When Do I Talk to Pooh-bah?

Below you will find a list of the most probable reasons for crossing paths with your ex. Guesstimate how much time you logged last month on each subject or event and record those figures in the space to the left. To the right, rate the level of communication stress using the following 4-point scale.

0=Never stressful
1=Occasionally
2=Frequently
3=Almost always

Talk Time with Pooh-bah Last Month	Subject/Event	Stress Level
_____	To make visitation arrangements	____
_____	Drop-off and pickup days	____
_____	Short, late, or absent child support	____
_____	School issues and events; extracurricular activities	____
_____	Child's medical care	____

Talk Time with Pooh-bah Last Month	**Subject/Event**	**Stress Level**
_____	Legal matters	____
_____	He called to speak with your child and you picked up the phone first	____
_____	Talking about getting back together/reconciliation	____
_____	Other	____
_____	Other	____
_____	Total time	

You probably spend less time talking to Pooh-bah each month than you do talking to the clerks in the grocery store, don't you? You made a baby with him; you have to talk to him occasionally. I'm sorry. But don't forfeit your sanity over a few minutes a month.

Exercise 2: Why I Don't Want to Talk to Pooh-bah

Finish the following statements by writing the first thing that comes to mind.

1. When I think about talking to my ex, I want to

2. When I hear his voice,

3. Most of the time, talking to him is like

4. My least favorite part of talking to him is

5. I feel like _____ when he says something annoying.

6. The worst conversation we ever had was over

7. When it was over, I remember wishing

8. We often have trouble communicating about

   discipline issues because

   he's pro-spanking and I'm not _____

   _____

9. Sometimes I avoid talking to him by _not answering_

   the phone because _often our conversations go_

   nowhere & I want to scream _____

   _____

10. I wish I could feel more _power_ when we talk:
    (positive emotion or behavior)

    _joy_____   _____

    _____   _____

    _____   _____

    _____   _____

    _____   _____

    _____   _____

Exercise 3: Bon Voyage, Bad Talks

You may want to tape the following passage or read it through several times before you do it:

Close your eyes and count backward from 25 to 1, breathing deeply and relaxing each part of your body by imagining a warm, blue liquid passing through it. When you reach the number 1, picture yourself on the deck of a luxurious cruise ship with the words *Goddess II* inscribed boldly at the bow. You're wearing your favorite outfit, hair done up just the way you like, looking out at the deep aqua ocean. Take in the scent of the ocean as you feel the sun warm on your skin . . .

. . . and then, taking all the time you need, turn around and notice the old, tattered trunk at the other side of the deck. When you walk over and open it, inside lies an anchor and one tiny note that reads: "Load me with your bad memories and fears of talking to your ex, and I will take them to the bottom of the deep blue sea."

Now begin thinking of all the ugly talks and anxiety around future ugly talks—many of those you retrieved in Exercise 1—and allow those images to flow into the trunk like a stream of stardust. Take all the time you need, or go as quickly as you can, putting every negative communication experience and old thought that would keep you from constructive conversations with your ex into the trunk. When you're all done, attach the anchor to the trunk, and slip it effortlessly over the side of the boat to the ocean bottom.

In the same time it has taken the old chest to sink, a shiny, new chest arises in its place. When you open it, images of all the positive emotions and behaviors you'd like to have when you talk to him come pouring out in another stardust stream into your heart.

Affirmations

1. I am willing to talk to my ex about things that concern our child.
2. I release my old resistance and negative ways of communicating with him.
3. I am willing to communicate with him in wonderful, new, positive ways.

14. STREAMLINE YOUR COMMUNICATIONS

It's 3:58 P.M. and 28-year-old Marta is putting the finishing touches on a sales report that is due on her boss's desk at 4:30. The minute she delivers it, she will have to grab her coat and race to her 3-year-old son's day care to pick him up by 5:00 P.M.

The receptionist buzzes in. Her ex-husband is on line 2. Last week he called her at work threatening to petition for full custody, and the conversation went downhill from there. What should Marta do?

  A. Ask her receptionist to take a message, and return his call later at a more convenient time.
  B. Ask her receptionist to take a message, and return his call as soon as she picks up her son.
  C. Take his call.

Okay, next one.

Brr-inggg, Brr-inggg. The clock reads 5:30 A.M., and it's not a dream, it's your phone. You wipe the sleep crust from one eye so you can read your caller ID. It's Pooh-bah. It's a school day, he's not scheduled to be with the children for three days, and at this hour you are more vampire than rooster. Do you:

  A. Turn the phone off and roll back over to sleep.
  B. Prop yourself on your elbow and wait for the message light to come on so you can check to see what he wants.
  C. Pick up the phone.

And one more:

Pooh-bah comes to pick up your child for the weekend and asks her to wait in the car (with his girlfriend) because he wants to talk to you about modifying the child support order. It will only take 10 minutes, he says, but you are scheduled for a hair appointment in half an hour and you are still in sweats and have not yet brushed your teeth. Do you:

A. Walk him to the door, lean in really close to him, and breathe out, "I've got an appointment. Let's talk later."
B. Ask for a few details, and if he's insistent, put off your hair appointment.
C. Immediately call your stylist to see if you can re-schedule for later in the day, and hear what he has to say.

If you racked up three A's, treat yourself to a pampering break and then move on to the next section.

If you chose B or C, it's time to learn three tenets of prime-time communicating.

1. Talk with Pooh-bah during *your* prime time.
2. Shift to prime time for unplanned but important quickie talks.
3. Stall if you're not up to it.

Interacting Prime Time

When you're talking to people who still love you, you often have the luxury of half thoughts, slurred speech, and babble chat. And even at your worst hour, on your worst day, when you sound like Tildy, the town idiot, they patiently translate your strange incantations into English and pretend they really got it. But don't expect that kind of generosity from Pooh-bah.

"I don't ever remember him being so mean and insensitive

before," says 31-year-old Janelle, who is separated. "I've always stuttered when I'm nervous or exhausted. During the nine years we were married, he was very understanding and he gave me the time I needed to get out what I was trying to say, but now he finishes my sentences in a hurry and then laughs at me."

When you're too tired, testy, blue, disoriented, rushed, brain-scrabbled, or depleted to string coherent sentences together, lay low. Otherwise, your ex might use those small seeds of vulnerability, ambiguity, hostility, or senility to grow a fit too.

In general, the higher your stress and his stress over a particular subject, the more prime-time you should be. For example, schedule talks about any subject you listed in Exercise 1: When Do I Talk to Pooh-bah? (page 78), for which you rated your stress level at 2 (frequently stressed) or 3 (almost always stressed) during prime time.

Now, let's figure out when your prime times are, so you can make better use of these windows. Consider your energy flow through a typical day, week, and month, and playacting aside, circle at least three of the times below. Or add your own times that represent your most confident, alert, clearheaded, energetic, diplomatic, unshakable, invincible, or joyful periods.

• Morning	• Beginning of the month
• Afternoon	• Middle of the month
• Evening	• End of the month
• Weekends	• Spring
• Before a massage	• Summer
• Before dinner	• Autumn
• Before a vacation	• Winter
• After exercise	• _____
• After church	• _____
• After pampering	• _____

Shifting to Prime Time

If Pooh-bah corners you at your children's school after an event or during a visitation pickup or drop-off that's normally a hi-and-bye and says he wants to talk about something "important," and you're feeling more like Tildy than a goddess, you can upgrade for a brief chat by using the 10-minute masquerade. But before you shape-shift, find out what he wants to talk about if you don't already know, and if you don't sniff a smidgen of urgency, stall (next section). If you do, excuse yourself momentarily and take brisk strides to the nearest bathroom (because it's one of the few places he can't follow you and interfere with your preparation). If you're on the phone, put him on hold or offer to call him back in 10 minutes.

When you get to the bathroom, apply lipstick and use the 30-second shift discussed in chapter 7 (page 52). Then return to the room and have a focused 1- to 10-minute chat, unless you feel like Julia Roberts and find you can stay in character longer. If you run out of steam before you've resolved anything, reschedule for your next anticipated prime-time moment.

Besides bathroom breaks, if you're alone with Pooh-bah in a public place and you need a time-out, check your voice mail, make pretend calls, or have a friend rescue-buzz you on your cell phone. The following aren't real numbers, mind you, but I have been known to break away from Pooh-bah, home in on the nearest pay phone, and pretend to call 1-800-GET-REAL, 1-800-CRAZYEX, and 1-800-HELPNOW.

It doesn't matter who you call, or pretend to call, the main thing is to put some distance between you and him for a few minutes if you are at risk of withering or pouncing on him and shaking him until his eyeballs fall out.

Stalling

You don't have to talk every time Pooh-bah wants to talk. Puh-lease. He may have the right to free speech, but you have the right to self-preservation. So if you're not in prime time, and he wants to talk about something shy of life-altering, stall.

When 32-year-old B.J.'s mother died of a sudden heart attack one December, her ex, who knew about her mother's death, relentlessly left messages on her voice mail several days after the funeral saying he needed to talk to her right away about the particulars of their 9-year-old's summer stay with him. *Summer vacation.* B.J. returned his call the following week, no harm done, when she was slightly less weepy.

Your life doesn't even have to be that bleak for a stall. Thirty-nine-year-old Carol rarely has lengthy conversations with her ex when she's overloaded at work by day or mothering her two preteens by night, when she's menstruating, or when she just knows he wants to prattle on about something trivial, stupid, or requiring her to perform extensive emotional aftercare on herself.

Here are three stall tactics:

1. The "Other Pressing Business" stall
   "I have to head out now for an appointment across town. I'll call you later and we'll talk." (*Note:* "Later" is your next anticipated prime-time moment.)

2. The "Sick" stall
   "I have a really bad flu/cold/strep throat (some contagious ailment), but this is important (whether it is or not), so let's talk when I'm over it so I don't infect you." (*Note:* If you're on the phone, start coughing like you're hacking up your lungs, or go nasal.)

3. "The Children Need Me Now" stall

In person: *"Jimmy's giving a speech in World History tomorrow and I told him I'd be his practice audience, so I'd best be on my way now."*

On the phone: *"Wow, I think Sharon's trying to wash Lindsey's hair with Lysol again. I have to go."* Click.

If he presses for "now" talk, cut it short. Get out of the room or off the phone with "I'm going to hang up now [or leave], but I'll call you." Say it politely, and then take care of yourself and go.

Affirmations

1. I value my time and I make loving choices about when to interact with my ex.
2. I am learning to shift to a productive talk time state whenever I choose to.
3. Every moment, I am aware of what I want to say or do to protect myself.

15. Try a Little Charm

It's Monday morning, you're driving to work in gridlock traffic, and you need to scoot over to the right lane so you can exit. The last two people ahead of you who tried to merge were unsuccessful. Do you:

A. Propel your car over, forsaking bumper and head-lights.
B. Stop where you are, face forward, stalling all the cars behind you until someone lets you over.
C. Turn to smile warmly and finger-wiggle wave to the next driver in that lane who could let you in.

Road rage being what it is today, I hope you chose C.

On the Pooh-bah expressway, a smile, a nod, a wink, or any act of kindness that might make him think you're about to lock arms with him and burst into The Lord's Prayer can multiply your odds of a breezy merge too.

What's that? You would rather staple your tongue than schmooze with Pooh-bah? Okay, but you don't have to let him know that every time you see him. It's time for another quiz. Which one of the following behaviors will help you enlist his cooperation?

A. Eyeball rolling
B. Glaring
C. Grunting
D. Screaming
E. Finger wagging
F. Chicken-neck gyrations
G. Bang fixing
H. Nail filing
I. Lipstick applications
J. All of the above
K. None of the above

Far be it from me to imply that you are actually doing any of the above (except K), or regularly behaving in any other ways that say "you are the scum of the earth" while talking to him. But if you are, it's not helping your cause. He is much more likely to work with you if he thinks he somehow ranks higher than tongue stapling and that you are willing to be somewhat polite. *Capisce?* Here are some quick ways to install this mirage.

1. On first contact, meet him with relaxed, smiling, I-know-this-is-hard-but-let's-do-the-best-we-can eyes.
2. Subtly imitate one positive or neutral aspect of his behavior for a few minutes while you're exchanging greetings and warm-up chitchat about nothing you'll ever remember.

For example, if he crosses his legs, you cross yours. If he points to something, you point to it too. If he makes a quizzical face, you copy. If he speaks slowly, slow your flow down to match his. This hypnotic pacing will help create an invisible link between the two of you, which will make him more receptive to your mind-meld, and the ensuing talk.

Note: If you're on the phone, match his tone and speed, repeat parts of every other thing he says, and respond with "um-hum," "okay, good," and "I see."

3. Once you feel in sync with him (one to three minutes), start into the real conversation using the Pooh-bah Power Talk model in the next section.

Affirmations

1. I can be pleasant to other people while still being powerful.
2. I'm willing to spend time putting him at ease if it will help me get what I want.
3. Charm and good graces become me.

16. Present Your Ideas in a Clear, Orderly Manner

Once you've bonded a little, you're ready to move on to the main course, the *Pooh-bah Power Talk*, which goes something like this:

1. *Choose an objective.* Determine what you want to accomplish, and work with it until it fits into one of these categories: (1) making a request or (2) sharing information. Notice, I did not say making a "complaint" or sharing a "tantrum."
2. *Keep yourself centered, and recenter as needed.* Do deep breathing, repeat a comforting prayer or affirmation, or use any of the grounding techniques discussed in Part I to keep yourself mellow.
3. *Tell him what you want in a coherent way.* Limit your talks to one or two issues at a time, and state your wishes in specific, easy-to-understand sentences so there will be no mistake about what you want.
4. *Handle objections and interruptions (if any).* Point out the biggest benefits this particular thing has to your child or to him.
5. *Reinforce the initial topic.* The best reinforcement is a summary of what he'll get out of cooperating. For example:

"You'll have more time with Susan if you arrive on time."
"If you set up a direct deposit for Marilyn's dance tuition, you won't have to mail a check every month and risk being late."

"It would be easier for us to talk to each other if we could both remember to take a few deep breaths and start over whenever we run into rough spots."

When you're dealing with an ex who has a history of noncompliance, supply motivating, negative consequences or alternative ways you will care for yourself and your child if he fails to comply.

"If you are late again on Friday, I'll have to take Susan with me to my aerobics class, and though I know it's out of your way, you will have to pick her up there or see her some other time."

"Pay Marilyn's tuition next week, with the late fee, or she won't be able to perform in the next recital, and you know how disappointed she'll be that you didn't follow through."

"If you keep calling me names, I'll leave."

Now, to show you how to put it all together, here are two Pooh-bah Power Talks from start to finish.

TARDY TAD

Forty-two-year-old Susan's ex-husband, Tad, is almost always late for his visitation weekends with their preteens. "He wears a watch, he's got a clock in the car, and a cell phone. And yet, even though he's supposed to pick up the kids at 6:30 P.M., most of the time he doesn't make it over until 7:30 or 8:00 P.M., without so much as a courtesy call. When I complain, he says I'm the one with the problem, even though the kids are clearly disappointed. Last week, when he wandered over later than ever, I threatened to take him out into the woods and hunt him for sport if he didn't get his act together."

Objective: To request promptness or a courtesy call if he is going to be late picking up the children.

One Hour Prior to Their Meeting

To center herself, Susan spends 15 minutes of focused deep breathing before her altar, visualizing herself remaining calm during her talk with Tad before meeting him at a neighborhood coffee shop. If irritation mounts at any point during the conversation, she can journey (page 42) or silently chant "relax."

The Meeting

Once Susan establishes rapport by greeting him with a warm smile and handing him some recent pictures of the children, she remains standing as he does, folds her hands behind her back to match his, and begins:

Susan, making a request: I'd like to talk to you about picking up the children on time when it's your weekend, or calling to say you're going to be late or aren't coming.

Pooh-bah (eyes slightly bulging with that here-she-goes-again look): What difference does it make if I'm late? You're always home anyway. If you didn't live out in the boonies, and they weren't always working on the roads, I'd be on time.

Susan, thinking about a sitcom she enjoyed the night before, points out the benefits of her request to the children and to Pooh-bah: The children really enjoy spending time with you, and they would have more time with you if you came at 6:30 P.M. They would worry less too. Last time you were over an hour late and Carol wanted me to call the police to see if you'd been in an accident, because I guess you promised her you wouldn't be late again. Did she tell you?

Pooh-bah: No . . . well . . . um . . . that's kind of extreme *(but he looks concerned).* She knows I'm going to be there. Sometimes I lose track of the time. *(He unfolds his hands and so does Susan as she points suggestively to two chairs. He sits and so does she.)*

Susan (with an innocent, but concerned look): Yes, I know it's silly, and I don't like bringing it up, but I know how much you love her and want her to be happy. Maybe if you came at 6:30 P.M. sharp for the next month she would settle down. Can you do that for her?

Pooh-bah: Okay (shrug).

Susan (last step, reinforcing his agreement to comply with her request): Okay then. I'll tell Carol that you'll be there to pick her and her brother up at 6:30 P.M. on Friday. Thank you.

Note: When Pooh-bah relents, always say thank you, even if you feel he should no more be thanked for the thing than for brushing his teeth.

Had Pooh-bah not relented, Susan could have repeated her request a few more times, changing the words ever so slightly, or moved to a negative consequence such as: *"The children asked about going to movie night at the school with their friends next Friday, so if you don't show or call by 7:00 P.M., I'm going to drop them off."*

RUBBER CHECK ROBERT

Jennifer, the soft-spoken 28-year-old mom of 6-year-old Michael, has been divorced for three years. When she's talking to Robert, her ex, he often interrupts or talks over her, and she feels like she's not being heard or respected. Her bank has just notified her that Robert's last child support check bounced.

Objective: To tell him the check bounced and request legitimate funds. Jennifer often crumbles on sight with her ex— shoulders slunked forward, eyes down, mousy voice—so she's going to playact by imitating her favorite TV lawyer to boost her feelings of power and confidence. If her façade begins to fade, she can request a bathroom break to refocus. And when the conversation ends, she will hightail it to a private place and journey to her favorite vacation spot.

The Meeting

When she arrives at Pooh-bah's office (where she's arranged to meet him, because he's less likely to make a scene over his rubber check if his coworkers are within earshot), he is slightly smirking. She greets him confidently as her favorite TV lawyer would, compliments him on his shirt, and then starts in:

Jennifer, sharing information: I dropped in to see you because your check bounced. Would you—

Pooh-bah (closing his office door and moving almost nose-to-nose with her): No, it didn't! What are you trying to pull!

Jennifer (maintaining relaxed eye contact and showing him the "Insufficient Funds" stamp on the back of his check as a visual aid): I'm sure it's just a mistake on their part. I was—

Pooh-bah (snatching the check, stepping back a few paces, and putting one hand on his hip, grumbling): Yeah, it was their fault, all right.

Jennifer (stepping back a few paces, putting one hand on her hip, and nodding her head vigorously in agreement while finishing her thought): I was planning to shop for Michael's fall clothes this weekend. Could you call your bank so I can resubmit the check?

Pooh-bah: Yeah (*weaker grumble*) . . . I'll call now. I might have to transfer funds if they can't figure out where they made the mistake. Wait in the lobby.

Jennifer: Thank you. (*Exits and half-skips to the water fountain, smiling to herself and humming, "I'm bad, I'm bad, you know it!"*)

Pooh-bah (comes out a few minutes later, stands over her in her lobby chair, hands her the check, and almost whispers): It's done. They're expecting you.

Jennifer (standing up and reinforcing her initial topic): Thank you. I'll resubmit the check after I pick Michael up from school.

Note: If her ex was uncooperative, Jennifer could have offered a negative consequence such as: "If you don't clear things up with your bank so I can resubmit the check or deliver the funds to me by the end of the day, I'm going to have your payroll checks garnisheed in the future."

I hope, with practice, you too will find yourself humming as you bop away from Pooh-bah. But even if that doesn't happen right away, as long as you select prime-time moments, slip in a little charm, and stick with the Pooh-bah Power Talk formula, your conversations with Pooh-bah will get better and better.

Along with patience and persistence, have compassion for yourself. All of this relentless conniving and manipulation is hard work. Turn up the pampering, and if for some reason any of your Power Talks turn into a poop talk, and you have passed your limit of civility, run to the nearest exit, rent a funny movie, pick up takeout, draw a goddess bath, and try it again another day.

Affirmations

1. I present my ideas in a clear, orderly manner.
2. I am convincing and persuasive.
3. I am willing to be a creative and flexible communicator.
4. I get what I want.

17. Put Words into His Mouth

When making requests of your ex, be sure to ask the questions or make the statements that are likely to produce the best results, namely, the ones that presuppose the answer. In other words, slide the answer you'd like to hear into the question, and be specific. If you'd like something done, mention a date, time, and/or a place. When possible, give one or two options that will alternately lead to what you want, so it seems like he has a choice. For example, with an ex who's always late, without giving you a courtesy call:

"Please bring Kira back at 6:00 P.M. on Sunday or call by 5:00 P.M. if you're going to be late."

will generate better results than:

"Bring Kira back on Sunday at a reasonable time."

With an ex who has been promising to buy your son's soccer shoes for weeks, try:

"Would you buy John's soccer shoes and drop them, or the money for me to buy them, on Saturday?"

instead of:

"Would you buy John's soccer shoes already?"

When you want to solicit your ex's help for improving your child's grades, try:

"Let's meet right after the parent conference on Thursday to create a plan to help Cathy improve her geometry grade."

instead of:

"Can we get together to talk about Cathy's geometry grade?"

Worst-case scenario: He'll look at you strangely, like

you've got two heads, and loop around or decline. Then you can suggest another option or find another way of taking care of yourself and your child. At least you'll find out quickly what he is willing to do.

Best-case scenario: He'll comply.

Your Turn

Practice the word-shoveling technique you've just learned by writing out requests in either question or statement form for the following dilemmas:

1. You want your ex to serve your child less junk food.
2. You want your ex to stop smoking in front of your child.
3. Your child has recently told you that her dad's seat belts don't work, so she's never buckled in.
4. You'd like your ex's honey to stop parking in your neighbor's driveway.
5. Your ex frequently allows your child to stay out, or up, until all hours of the night.

Affirmations

1. I am willing to help him become a better communicator and follow through on his commitments.
2. Every day, in every way, my ex is becoming more co-operative.
3. I work toward the best outcome.

18. Write Letters, Leave Phone Messages

If you're not yet the type who is so heavily into playacting that it's scary, letters and phone messages can be a wonderful thing. Lynda, a 36-year-old divorcée, prefers letter writing when she's sharing information about her 9-year-old with her ex. "Whenever we're face-to-face and he mentions his pig-dog wife who he was dating while we were still married, my hand starts twitching and I can't get the words out right after that. But I'm a lot more level-headed on paper, so I write." If you want to spare yourself a little live agony sometimes, and can frame your message as either a request or information sharing, say it in a letter.

For the most part, your letter should be written as a personable paper Power Talk, listing a precise, clearly stated objective, benefits for him and your child if you are making a request, and/or negative recourse if he doesn't cooperate. Use as few words as possible.

To elicit maximum cooperation, plug in positive words and phrases he's been known to respond to favorably and gross exaggerations of his goodness, as well as any of the following:

Your child's name	Please
Help/support	Thank you
An opportunity for you to	Grateful
Appreciate	Best/better
Good	I know

For example:

Request Letter, with Benefits and a Dash of Guilt

Dear Ken,

Carol was heartbroken the other day when you were over an hour late picking her up. She cried and paced back and forth for I don't know how long, watching for your car, and she wouldn't even eat dinner.

Ken, you're Carol's hero and she *loves* spending time with you. She's always bubbling over when she returns. I know you enjoy your time together too, and I want you to continue to have such good times.

Would you please come at 6:00 P.M. next Friday so her "before" is just as good as her "after"?

Thank you.

Shanti

P.S. Here's a new picture of Carol.

Announcement Letter

Dear Ricardo,

Frances's school is having an Open House on Friday, Feb. 4, from 6 to 9 P.M. All of her teachers will be there and I know you'd like to have an opportunity to meet them and tour her school. Dinners are available for $6.

Carmen

P.S. Frances will be one of the student tour guides and she'd love to show you around!

Keep in mind that you shouldn't send every letter you write. If, when you read your letter over, there is smoke rising from the paper, go for a walk, dance around your living room, mow the lawn, write a flaming I-HATE-YOUR-GUTS letter in your Small Thoughts journal, or paint your toenails until the nasty oozes out of you. Then try again, remembering that the purpose of your letter is to share information or make a request, and that it's best to keep it short and to the point (one page is fine).

You should also omit condescending instructions (e.g., "Feed the children before 7:00 P.M.," "Comb Karen's hair," and "Make sure Martin puts his shoes on the right feet"). And tempting as it may be to call him names like rat brain, evil one, and Neanderthal, you should avoid using those too.

Enough about what you shouldn't do. Here's what you should do: Write the letter on personal stationery and, perhaps, include a current picture of your child, one of her drawings, or some other heart-softening token. Stick to a journalistic format if announcing an event: Who? What? When? Where? How? Stick with the facts, and sprinkle your child's name throughout the letter.

It may take a few drafts to get your letter right, but remember, you want results, so take the time to tone it down if you need to. Here are a few made-over sections of flame letters.

1. When your ex repeatedly brings your daughter home late, causing you to scramble to get her to soccer practice, and you really want to write,

When you brought Alexi home yesterday, it may have been 2 o'clock in Oz, but it was 3:00 P.M. here, and we were late for soccer practice . . . AGAIN. Do we need to have our parenting order modified to say American Pacific Standard Time?

scribble this instead:

Alexi's soccer coach says she's going to have to run extra laps if she's late again, and I know you wouldn't want her to have to do that, so would you please drop her off at 2:00 P.M. sharp so she can get to practice on time?

2. When your ex has been prodding your child to call his girlfriend "Mommy" and you really want to write,

> Darren told me you asked him to call your whorish-girl-friend-who-you-were-probably-sleeping-with-before-we-got-divorced "Mommy," and I'm sure you grew even dumber after you said it, and no way is it going to happen.

scribble this instead:

> I know you want Darren to bond with Sharon, but he feels uncomfortable calling her "Mommy." I'm sure you understand the conflict, and will continue to support him in calling her Sharon.

Phone Messages

Have you ever just wrapped up a conversation with your ex, relieved to no end to be on your way somewhere he wasn't, only to realize you forgot one teensy-weensy little detail? Or needed to relay a 30-second snip of info and did not under any circumstances want to see his face or hear any feedback? Try leaving info bites, reminders, and confirmations on his voice mail or answering machine.

To make doubly sure he doesn't pick up the phone and spoil your mischief, call while he's at work, when you know he's out and about with the children, when he's out of town, or just after he's pulled out of your driveway.

Affirmations

1. I make ample use of letters and phone-message technology.
2. Clarity and ingenuity flow through me in each way I choose to communicate.
3. Even when I'm upset over the subject matter, I can still be graceful and express myself in a purposeful way.

19. BRAKE A BULLY

If Pooh-bah is a rottweiler, Pooh-bah the bully is Cujo with a blood sugar imbalance, and he brings additional drama to the goddess communication proposition. He rants, he raves, he growls and grimaces, and he, unlike plain Pooh-bah, is not so easily swayed by a warming whiff of humanity and good manners. In fact, if it were legal, he might be more responsive to a few quick zaps with a cattle prod than a cold-turkey Power Talk. Then again, he's not beyond reach. Not if you can distract and sedate him first.

Distraction and Sedation

This is a deliberate, respectful three-step process of taking the bite out of a bully so you can then have a constructive Power Talk with him. You can move into your Power Talk after any step that creates this window for you.

1. Assume the following body language:

Eyes: steady, relaxed gaze, making frequent eye contact
Head: still and straight
Hands: still or purposeful, moving smoothly, or at sides
Voice: relatively soft, flat and impassive, yet self-confident

2. Without letting on that you're put off, listen and watch him for a couple of minutes so you can cali-

brate the level of intervention required. If he's frothing over something you want to do anyway, regardless of the bullying, agree to it and end the conversation.

3. Casually interject totally unrelated topics in a natural but Mr. Magoo sort of way, using sentences with no more than six words having fewer than six letters. Don't worry about spilling over a little and don't be obvious about your count as you speak. It's even better if you break his thought pattern with off-the-subject phrases containing positive or desirable behaviors. Here are a few examples:

"Hmmm . . . the dog is quiet."
"The breeze is just right today."
"What a calm night."
"The cat looks relaxed, huh?"
"Praise God."

Most likely, the first three bizarre offerings will disengage him, but if not, try a few more and make them more personal. "I saw your mom today." "Don't you love our boy's laugh?" (Remember, six short words or less to a sentence.)

Should he continue misbehaving, just stand there and witness (page 43) for a minute or two, with a blank Spock face (page 53). If he's got a conscientious bone left in his body, he'll be too embarrassed to continue and will adjust his attitude, but if he doesn't, leave the room to give him an extended period of time to reflect on his immature behavior.

If my friend Jill's Energizer-bully ex is on the warpath for more than five minutes, she feigns a look of despair, puts the back of one hand to her forehead like she's just remembered some pressing obligation, and excitedly says something like, "Man . . . hold on, I have to call Nailah back," as she's walking out of the room. Then she picks up the phone and *really* calls me to chat for about 10 minutes. He almost always winds down before she gets off the phone, but if he's anything shy of Milquetoast, she asks him to leave.

If you want a firsthand glimpse of the power thought disruption can have to break down hostility before you try it out on Pooh-bah, instruct a friend to interrupt you over and over this way the next time you're a little crazed.

A Few Other Things to Keep in Mind When Conducting a Bully Intervention

1. *Have a sense of adventure and a sense of humor.* If you saw a Pooh-bah-like actor on the rampage on your favorite sitcom, wouldn't you be curious to see what stupid thing he was going to do or say next, and wouldn't you have a few laughs? Laugh at yours too.
2. *Be flexible enough to keep adjusting your behavior until he relinquishes the attack.* You've got lots of variables to play with whenever you're interacting with a bully. Change your body language, change the tone of your voice, rattle off non sequiturs, leave the room. If one doesn't seem to slow him down, try another. By remaining flexible, you'll remain in charge.
3. *Step up the pampering.* Select at least two of the most nourishing treats from your master pampering list after each bully intervention.

Affirmations

1. I am able to communicate easily with difficult people.
2. I become even calmer and more persuasive when others are out of control.
3. I care for myself after each upset.

20. Hear No Gossip, Defend No Gossip

"With my ex, it was one low ball after another for almost a year after we first separated. He told mutual friends I cheated on him. He told his coworkers I worshiped Satan. He told his dad that my piano instructor was our youngest son's father. But the most hurtful thing he ever did was tell our boys' day care provider that I beat them when they mentioned his name," says 39-year-old Denise. "I didn't even know about his latest smear campaign until I picked the boys up at the day care one day and she handed me a pamphlet labeled "Don't Hit, Don't Hurt," a sort of step program for abusive parents.

"I didn't know what to say, and suddenly I was crying and rushing the boys out to the car. After three years of taking care of them, she should have known I'd never do such a thing. I spent almost an hour on the phone with her the next morning trying to convince her that he was lying, but I could tell she still thought it was true, so I've never taken the boys back."

Your ex's friends, new honeys, relatives, coworkers, and assorted busybodies may form negative opinions about you because of his lies. Some of your very own Benedict Arnold friends might even be turned. So what, so what, so what? Do you want to be the gossip police or a goddess? As the gossip police you, like our friend Denise above, would actually scurry around denying or deconstructing his stories and most likely end up morbidly depressed and drained from the effort. However, as a goddess, you wouldn't think twice about commenting on any of these whirly-twirly nit-nats.

You'd act like you had a hearing problem whenever someone passed on ex gossip to you. And when that didn't stop the more incessant, nosy slug-worm meddlers from attempting to get a rise out of you, you'd try one of these lines from my Gossip Tolerance Program (GTP).

1. "I have nothing to say about that." (Delivery: Maintain direct eye contact; don't blink, twitch, or appear shocked.)
2. "Hmmm, I see." (Cock your head slightly to one side, and with an innocent, tsk-tsk-gossiping-is-so-second-grade look, ask) "Wouldn't the world be a better place if we got our information from the source?"
3. "What would you say if I told you someone who was mad at you lied about you?"
4. "What would make you believe something like that about me?" (Point to your heart, tear up a little, and hold the "me.")
5. "It's not true." (Then change the subject.)
6. "He's going through a rough time right now, and he's lashing out in every way possible. I know this is difficult for you too, but I'm trying to work through this in a very private way." (This line is especially for mutual friends, school officials, and day care providers.)

Affirmations

1. I hold my own truths sacred.
2. I am willing to allow others to form their own opinions.
3. The people who love me support my gossip-free lifestyle.

21. BE DISCREET ABOUT YOUR PRIVATE LIFE

"I just don't understand why he refused," one 25-year-old divorced mom lamented during the '97 NGAWYEM campaign, "when I asked him if we could switch weekends with the girls, because I wanted to fly down to Hawaii with my boyfriend for a business trip."

She really didn't. But I hope you do. Her mission was to switch weekends, not give him the 411 on her love life. If she had omitted the offending noun "boyfriend" and maybe been a bit vague about her destination, supplying a 1-800 pager number or her parents' number in case of emergencies, I'm sure she would have been stuffing her suntan lotion, swimsuit, sunglasses, and sarong into her suitcase instead of talking to me. I'm not suggesting you lie, but like my good friend's favorite aunt Delia used to say, *"Don't go spilling all of your guts to anybody. Always keep a little something to yourself."*

Being tight-lipped is a little tricky with exes, because when you get them in the right light and you see a once-loved expression on their face, despite their recent snaggletoothed behavior, you can find yourself rattling on about intimate details of your new life like you kinda still love them.

Because Pooh-bah and I had been friends forever before we became lovers and married, and the Pollyanna-me hoped we could return to being best buds right after the divorce, I saw him more than I should have and told him more of my business than necessary too. And it was not a

good thing for his ego, because he immediately and cor-
rectly surmised that my life was going on without him. I invited him to several private picnics, attended a few of his
work parties with Esprit, and even said yes when he asked
me to work for him one summer. He was managing a print
shop, and he wanted me to be the onsite computer specialist and writer. I rightfully hesitated at first, but because
we have always jibed creatively I thought we could do it; I
thought it would be a nice tribute to our collective creative
genius. I was also in between jobs and surely I'd get child
support on time if I was right under his nose every day.

Really, that was my logic.

Alma called me every five minutes to talk me out of it,
but we managed to work together for two months. Neither
one of us talks a lot while working, but during the course
of any day, between customers and orders, I sporadically
interjected thoughts about my seven favorite subjects: Esprit, yoga, pampering, *Star Trek*, sunshine, beaches, and the
color purple. He listened, and shared too. We laughed occasionally, and once he, his girlfriend, and I even had lunch
together.

But then one fateful day I told him about my new massage therapist's magic fingers. He happened to be gay, but
before I could share that part with Pooh-bah, he squared
his eyes on me like I had just crawled out of the sewer and
all of our subsequent conversations that day mysteriously
looped back to our divorce. The spell was broken, and our
working relationship was shot to hell, so I collected my last
paycheck and hit the road.

This might be my wild imagination in overdrive, but
since then, I've also noticed that certain taboo words alarm
him and make it more difficult to finish a conversation, so
I delete them from my vocabulary when I'm around him.
They include: 1992 (the year of our divorce); 1993 (the year
after our divorce); home; names of old neighborhoods;
names of old mutual friends; and male names.

Your ex probably has his no-no-I'm-going-to-go-ballistic-now trigger words and subjects too, and it would probably help to keep them out of your conversations, so why don't you take a few moments now to list them in the margin. Here are some tickler categories to get you started:

1. How happy you are without him
2. Current loves
3. Career advances, promotions, raises
4. Fun social activities
5. Future plans
6. Vacations
7. His bad behavior

So if you're not going to chat with your ex about your trip to Hawaii with your boyfriend, your favorite things, your dreams, and the richness of your life, what's left? Try any of these:

1. Subjects in Exercise 1: When Do I Talk to Pooh-bah (page 78)—except reconciliation because that was a sick joke
2. The weather
3. Y2K glitches
4. How to change the oil in your car (this is very important stuff, and most men know)
5. Idle chatter about nothing you'll ever remember

If you want to pour out your soul or carry on like someone slipped truth serum in your water, call a friend.

Affirmations

1. My life and my plans are precious, and I will share them with people who support me.

2. I am discreet.
3. I am willing to omit bothersome words and phrases in order to have more productive talks.

> *"Remember when life's path is steep to keep your mind even."*
>
> —Horace

Ritual #2

This is a good once-a-month ritual to help improve your communications with your ex even more.

What you will need:

- Index card
- Blue pen
- A space on your altar for the index card

Write down 10 ways your talks with your ex have improved this month, and then flip the card over and write 10 ways you want your talks to improve next month. Then, holding your card in the palm of one hand, with the other hand covering it, close your eyes and count backward from 25 to 1. Visualize your ex sitting before you, with a smiling, understanding look on his face. In your mind's eye, hand the card to him, and watch him look it over and then agree to work with you to accomplish these things. Before he fades from sight, listen as he tells you one more thing he is willing to do to make things easier for you. Then, in your own time, count back from 1 to 25, becoming more and more alert, feeling even more confident about your next talk with him. And when you reach 1, place the index card on your altar for a month.

PART 3

Visitation

"But I have promises to keep/and miles to go before
I sleep."
—Robert Frost

*The closer our first visitation day came, the more I won-
dered how I could possibly hand over the little love of my life
to the pig who had almost driven me to snort Tang. I just
didn't trust him. Not one bit. Would he feed her fresh veg-
etables, abstain from smoking around her, and braid her
hair or at least pat it down before he took her out in public
looking like Alfalfa's twin sister? Would he bring her back?*

*In time, after many, many torturous, self-induced
visitation-day anxiety attacks, after seeing her go away and
come back at least 100 times, happy and hair-combed, I
thought it wise to conclude that she never saw Pooh-bah,
just Daddy, and that all was well in her world.*

22. SHARE YOUR CHILD

Unless you can convince a family court judge that one of the following is true, you have a legal and moral obligation to share your child with your ex:

1. You are the second Virgin Mary in history, and your child has no father.
2. Your ex is not the father of your child.
3. He is a drug fiend, mobster, chain-saw murderer, or something along those lines.

Anything? Well, then you're going to have to share.

I know you would never do this sort of thing, but I once read about a man whose ex-wife turned out all of the house lights and hid in the garage with their two elementary-school-age children one Friday when he came to pick them up for his weekend. He didn't know they were in the garage until, on his way back to his car, he heard his son's small voice inquire, "Mommy, why are we hiding from Daddy?" She told him they were playing hide-and-seek, of course.

Outraged, the man went to the garage door and yelled, "Hey, I know you're in there!" but they never came out. Now, assuming he was not standing in the driveway with an electric chain saw, and it was his weekend, she was being very, very naughty.

Sharing Pays Off

Even though you may think your ex is a no-good snot and that nothing worthwhile could possibly come from your child spending more than five minutes with him, child sharing is an honorable thing to do, and it can enrich your life in many ways. It will keep the link open between your child and his father, giving them continuity and an opportunity to grow their love; it will help you build goodwill with your ex; it will give you parenting breaks; and it will prevent your ex from dragging your butt into court every other month for contempt.

Jerk of the first order or not, he still deserves his place in your child's life, and it can mean more than you know to your child. Here are a few testimonials from children of divorced parents who took the high road:

- *Brianne, 7:* "Saturday, Daddy takes me to my other house with him. We walk to the park, and sometimes we get ice cream in the summer, and he swings me in the swing and I laugh and laugh, and so does he."
- *Marco, 12:* "I know he makes fun of Mom sometimes and I hope that changes, but he comes to all of my soccer games and cheers the loudest when I make a goal."
- *Ramon, 20, third-year college student:* "Mom doesn't like Dad, but unlike many of my divorced friends' moms, she never makes me feel guilty about calling him for fatherly advice, or visiting him for one of my breaks instead of her."
- *Nicole, 34, proud new mother:* "I didn't even think twice about inviting Dad to the baby's christening too. I knew Mom would find a way to be gracious, and I wanted them both there."

Learning to Share

So how do you poke your lip back in and amiably share your child with Pooh-bah when you don't want to? Your legally filed visitation agreement is a good place to start. If you're like many parents, dividing your child into weekdays and weekends, holidays, and school vacations is an emotional odyssey that can suck to high heaven, but it will help simplify and restabilize your child's life, so do it. And if you don't already have a visitation agreement, here are a few tips to help you put one together immediately:

- *Keep it simple and clear.* There should be no statements like these in your visitation agreement. "On the fifth Sunday of every third year, child will spend time with so-and-so," or "Child will visit father every other Friday at 6:00 P.M. if she feels like it," or "Father will bring child home on Sunday evening before it gets dark." A good rule of thumb is to specify days and times of departure and return that will allow your children to spend regular "normal" time with their father, as well as alternate major holidays and school vacations.
- *Make it "child" friendly.* Divorced 29-years-olds Jenni and Joe evenly divided up their daughter Maura's week between the two of them. After a month, poor little 6-year-old Maura became so disoriented and burnt out from all the shuffling back and forth that she went from gregarious to grumpy. How would you like to try that routine? Don't create a schedule for your children that you couldn't keep up with yourself.
- *Get help if you need it.* If the two of you cannot map out a reasonable schedule that works for both of you and your child, enlist the help of an attorney or a mediator.

Once you have a visitation agreement, honor it. No double-booking a zillion extracurricular activities for the kids on your ex's time, or manipulatively steering them away from dad time. No coyly whining over Easter without them, if you got Christmas. No fabricated emergencies one hour before your ex shows up. If you lose out on favored dates or events, haggle politely. Who knows, if you ask nicely, and don't tell him you're going to Hawaii with your boyfriend, he might switch parenting weekends with you.

And if he gives a little, you give a little every now and then too. If some of the events in his life don't coincide with the visitation schedule, or he wants extra time with his child, work with him—especially if it's not disruptive, and you have no other plans for your child. As you must know through family, friends, talk shows, and eavesdropping on other people's conversations, a lot of dads drop out of their children's lives altogether. So when Pooh-bah, whom you may still hate, asks to take your child to a traveling circus that's only in town for four days, please lean toward a yes. Here are a few other times when you should consider saying yes to more time:

- Special events at work (holiday parties, family gatherings, award ceremonies)
- Special family events (anniversaries, weddings, reunions)
- Religious events
- Activities they both enjoy (chess championships, sporting events, etc.)
- Seasonal or once-in-a-lifetime cultural or historical events
- Educational activities (science fairs, book fairs, library presentations, SAT workshops, etc.)
- Fitness activities
- Father/child events

When Can You Say No to Too Much Sharing?

Thirty-five-year-old Cinnamon had a 7-year-old son, Benny, with her then-live-in boyfriend, Luke, who ran out on them while she was in the hospital giving birth. Luke recently moved back to town to develop a relationship with his son, whom Randy, her husband of six years, has helped her raise. "I'm still so angry and resentful toward him for abandoning us that I wish he'd disappear again, but now that the judge has just granted him supervised visitation every other Friday at my house (until Benny gets to know him), he's always trying to sneak over more."

One Saturday morning, he phoned at 5:30, as she was packing for a camping trip with Randy and Benny, to say he'd forgotten to drop off a gift for Benny the night before, and by the way, could he spend a few hours with him before they took off. He could come right over. She told him it wasn't a good time, but he pushed to come anyway, dangling the gift, and Randy lobbied for him because he was finally making an effort. "So, I gave in, and it ruined my vacation. There I was out in a beautiful rain forest with my two guys later that morning, and all I could think about was what a butthole Luke was for pushing his way into my house again." She could have responded to Luke's request like this instead:

> "This isn't a good time, we're so busy packing and things are all over the floor. Benny will be back in a few days, and the gift will keep until then. Got to go."

Whether your ex is a recovering drop-out dad or not, all impromptu demands for more time should be weighed against self-preservation and child preservation, so say no to more time if it's grossly inconvenient, upsetting, or depleting for you or your child.

Sustain Yourself While Your Child Is Gone

Thoughts of missing your children can often keep you from happily wanting to share them. It took me a couple of years to totally warm up to Esprit's twice-a-month sleepovers at her dad's, and I went through withdrawal every time she left. The first whole summer she was away with him, I ached so much without her, that on the tenth day I got in my car and drove out to get her. Fortunately, when I got there it was 5:46 on a Saturday morning, and I had the decency to drive myself back home without a knock or a whimper.

It's not like I didn't have friends, or things to do, or sleep to catch up on for that matter, but I missed her *that* much. After my 40-minute drive back home, I picked up a pad of paper and practiced writing with my left hand, something I'd been meaning to teach myself to do for years. And by noon, I was almost ambidextrous and feeling like I could at least make it through the rest of the day without her.

I know the quiet house your children leave behind on visitation days can be haunting—even though it is often an answered prayer—but what are you going to do while they're gone? You may have already thought of house-cleaning (boo), errand running (boo), bill paying (boo), but what about FUN, EXPANSION, and ah, yes, PAMPERING?

Another way to put the time your child is away to good use is to do simple things most childless people take for granted, such as:

- Sleep
- Watch adult movies
- Walk around naked
- Enjoy uninterrupted time in the bath or on the phone
- Go on a date
- Go out, period
- Eat Cheerios for dinner
- Sleep some more

Don't waste free time pining for your children. *They'll be back soon enough*. Whether it's a day, a weekend, a holiday vacation, or a whole summer, honor them, and honor yourself, by using that time well.

Affirmations

1. We easily share our child.
2. I enjoy having my child spend time with her father.
3. We schedule our child's time between us with ease.

23. Cut Down on Late Pickups, Drop-offs, and No-shows

Okay, you've wrapped your brain around this notion of sharing your children, worked out a visitation schedule, found something to do with yourself while they're away, and then lo and behold, Pooh-bah has the nerve throw the whole thing off by not following through on his end of the deal. He shows up late, or he forgets his days, or something comes up and he wants makeup days, or he decides to parent in absentia.

You sit there dumbfounded and brain sore that Pooh-bah, who manages to arrive at work and the barber shop on time, and plant his tail in front of the TV every year a half hour before the Super Bowl starts, could be late or a no-show for the very fruit of his loins.

The whole ordeal becomes even more mind-boggling when you know that he has a clock in his house and his car and a wristwatch; he fought for months in court to increase his visitation rights; he really enjoys spending time with little Johnny; and he swore last time he was late that it wouldn't happen again.

Then, why the Tardy Tad routine? Maybe he's a time-challenged, Special Needs drone, who will always be 2 to 20 minutes late for every other date in his life. Or, maybe this is a fluky, transitional adjustment to the dynamics of weekend fathering. Or, maybe he's purposely being totally irresponsible to yank your chain. Whatever the reason, these little tricks will help reduce tardiness, no-shows, and no-calls.

1. *Clarify their date a day or so in advance.* Phone and say something like "So you'll pick up (child's name) tomorrow at (time), and then you'll drop her off at (day/time)."
2. *Honor plans you've made regardless of whether or not he shows on time.* If your ex is an hour late (or whatever reasonable "late" time you've established) for your child, take her to the neutral zone (see page 130), or take her with you and leave a note on the door or a message on his phone machine for him to come back when you return. If he brings her home late and you're not there, give him the option of dropping your child off at the neutral zone, or returning with her when you're home.
3. *Share your child's disappointment.* Being stood up or scooped up late by your own parent bites, but your child might be reluctant to share his blue feelings with his father. You can fill in for your child by giving Pooh-bah the Tardy Tad Power Talk on page 93, or by simply saying something like "(Your child's name) feels sad (taken for granted, hurt, etc.) when you don't show up when you say you will, or call to say you'll be late, or don't show and don't reschedule."
4. Use motivating negative consequences such as:

"Gene wants to take a Saturday art class, and you haven't picked him up for a month, so I'm going to enroll him."
"My parents would like to spend time with Brooke this weekend too, so if you're not here by 7:00 P.M., I'll drop her off at their house."

If your ex often brings your child home two or more hours late without a courtesy call, and you have a legally filed visitation agreement, supply more motivating negative consequences. And then, if nothing changes, try the following:

1. Remind him for several months that you expect him to stick to the agreed-upon return time, pointing out

the benefits this will have to your child (time to settle in, do homework, have a relaxed dinner, take care of her chores, get proper rest, etc.). Then tell him that you will be doing something in X number of days if he does not improve his behavior.

2. Have a friend on hand for the drop-offs so you have a witness to his violation of your agreement.

3. If the extreme tardiness continues after the X-number-of-days amnesty period ends, here's a stop-tardiness method that worked for 26-year-old Karyn, whose ex brought their 3-year-old back hours, sometimes even a day, late for almost six months; it might work for you.

Call the police and tell them that your ex is in violation of your visitation agreement, that you're worried, and that you'd like help locating your child. Make sure you have a copy of your visitation agreement on hand when the officer arrives at your door.

Your ex will probably show up before the APB goes out, but if the least that happens is he gets home and finds a message on his voice mail from the police, you will have sent a clear message to him that his late days are numbered. He'll be pissed, of course, but it will pass, and you should not have to worry unnecessarily about your child's whereabouts, so if you've reached this point, just do it.

Affirmations

1. Every day, her father is becoming more sensitive to her feelings and more considerate of her needs.

2. I release the need to get upset when his father is late or does not show up at all.

3. I am willing to allow friends and family to be my visitation-day helpers.

24. Rule Your Own Castle

I have a no-shoes policy in my home, so I confiscate all footgear at the front door. Everyone happily complies, except Pooh-bah, who looks at me suspiciously each and every time I ask him to remove his shoes, like I just made up the rule for him. Then he usually declines, and because it's my home, I confine him to the hallway.

Eileen, a 26-year-old divorced nonsmoker, despises when her ex smokes in her house while he's waiting for their 13-year-old daughter to pack, and then doesn't even empty the ashtray. Where do you suppose he's getting the ashtray, and what's stopping her from extending her house no-smoking policy to him? She could have nipped his nicotine habit in her house in the bud by making a request, sharing information, or supplying a compelling negative consequence. For example:

Request: "Would you please smoke outside?"
Sharing information: "There is no smoking in my house."
Negative consequence: "If you light up in my house again,
    I'll ask you to leave."

And here's some help for 29-year-old China, whose ex flings the family cat from the love seat onto the floor and then claims her spot.

Request: "Please stop throwing the cat on the floor."

Sharing information: "That's the cat's spot. If she bothers you, you can sit over here."

Negative consequence: "If you throw the cat on the floor again, I'm going to throw you out."

Now it's your turn to practice stopping your ex from making himself overly comfortable in your home by using clear requests or information sharing and supplying negative consequences if you've told him the rules over and over and he's still unruly. So bring to mind something your ex does in your home that conflicts with your house rules that you'd like to stop and create several alternative cessation scripts.

Problem behavior: _____

_____

_____

Request: _____

_____

_____

Sharing information: _____

_____

_____

_____

_____

Negative consequence: _____

_____

_____

Setting the Mood

It can be so much easier to get Pooh-bah to behave in your home after you've lulled his anarchistic thoughts with some environmental tranquilizers. On most visitation days—and most ordinary days—my home smells of either lavender, sandalwood, or frankincense and myrrh. The holy scents merge with the sounds of piano music or soft jazz and float through the house. And if it's late fall, winter, or cold spring and there's no burning ban in effect, the crackle of a warm, raging fire in my living room joins the melody. Pooh-bah tries to resist its mesmerizing call, but it always pulls him. Once when he was over, and he'd surrendered his shoes at the door, I sat him on the couch and went to get him a glass of water. When I returned he was staring into the fire like a lovesick puppy.

If there's no fire, his eyes roam to the pictures on the walls of Esprit and me and the friends who love us, to the fresh flowers on the kitchen counter, and to my endless purple knickknacks. If ever I can count on invoking the spirit of Ex Charming, it's in my home.

Here are a few other ways to create a relaxing home ambience of your own so you can keep yourself and Pooh-bah tranquil:

1. Keep your home clean and uncluttered.
2. Sprinkle it with objects of beauty, joy, and peace, such as flowers, happy-face pictures, framed prayers, nature scenes, or balloons.

3. Diffuse incense, potpourri, or fragrant essential oils.

Setting Up a Neutral Pickup/Drop-off Zone for Your Children

If, after the incense and the soothing music, and the negative consequences of bad behavior, Pooh-bah is still too extreme in your home, have him pick up your children or drop them off at a neutral friend's or relative's house. You can also arrange for him to pick up your children from school, day care, work, or extracurricular activities.

Affirmations

1. My house is full of peace and love, and all who enter feel it.
2. I welcome my ex into my home, and he is the perfect guest.
3. I have the right to enforce my house rules.
4. Every day, it is easier and easier to share pleasant moments with my ex.

25. Invite Friends Over When You're Expecting Him

If you've ever noticed that your ex's brawl-starting tendencies increase when it's just the two of you, you might want to consider holding court when he's due.

Twenty-seven-year-old Jenni wanted to put an end to her ex's relentless nitpicking when he came to pick up their 10-year-old for the weekend, so she set up a Friday-night book club that coincidentally started the same time he was scheduled to arrive. "Was he surprised to find six women who were already in a pissy, skin-a-male mood, from reading our first book, *Waiting to Exhale*. He didn't say much and he didn't stay long."

Sandra, 31, calls her bodybuilder brother and his wife over to help her greet her troublemaking ex. You made a list in chapter 11 of people you could call on for assistance (see page 69). Does one of them look like a bodyguard or a kung-fu master? And while you're thinking about that, come up with at least one friendly gathering to host for your next Pooh-bah visit.

Besides offsetting the full impact of your ex's attacks, friends can also help keep you from committing Pooh-bah-cide. At least that's what 28-year-old Tina was hoping when she invited Jamal, the guy she was kind of seeing, to dinner with her ex and his new wife. She knew her ex wanted to talk about increasing his visitation with their twin 10-year-old boys, a sore topic for her, since he was a workaholic and the boys tended to end up with his wife while he was at the office. And she knew it was going to be a challenge to keep from telling him it would be a cold day in hell before that happened.

"Jamal's very diplomatic. I knew he'd be a relaxing, modifying influence, and I could count on him to kick me under the table if he saw my eyes rolling back into my head, which for me is the prelude to a verbal assault. With him beside me, I got through dinner without spilling drinks on my ex or insulting him, while politely refusing to agree to more time until he cut down on work."

Company might also be useful around the holidays, at school events, and at mediations and court hearings.

Affirmations

1. My friends are always near to support me.
2. I'm open to drawing strength from people who love me.
3. I am loved and protected.

26. DOWNPLAY YOUR EX'S BADMOUTHING TO YOUR CHILD

"What I cannot love, I overlook." —Anaïs Nin

Once when Esprit was 8, she came home from a weekend at Pooh-bah's, stroked my face, put her nose to mine, and quietly and solemnly, as if she'd still have loved me anyway, asked me if I was a lesbian. On other occasions, she's interrogated me about taking all her dad's money, not relaying his messages when he's stood her up, and sleeping around while she's visiting him.

From the distorted, distant look on her face and the proximity of her "dad" time, I can usually single out the mudslinger, and I have always responded to the "mud" reports much the same as I would anything the lizard-tail lady might have to tell me. Brush off, play off, and laugh.

And if I wouldn't tell the lizard-tail lady that she wasn't a reptile and therefore did not have a tail, because I thought she was a few marbles short of a bag or had felonious information, why would I go out of my way to convince Esprit that I wasn't a conniving, lying, money-grabbing, whorish lesbian? When Esprit was small, some of my comebacks to her mud reports went something like this:

1. Saying "hmmm" thoughtfully and letting it go.
2. Laughing (even when it wasn't funny).
3. Changing the subject. (This was especially effective when she didn't really understand what new words like "lesbian" and "whore" meant anyway.)
4. Reciting one of the following:

"Well, that's interesting."

"Thank you for sharing that."

"I might have a word with your father about that." (I didn't.)

Forty-six-year-old Carmen's ex had every-other-weekend visitation with their two preteen children after the divorce, and when the kids were with him, he scoffed at Carmen's parenting skills, the men she dated, and her poofy hair. Inevitably, the kids brought the ill praises home for rebuttal, and Carmen, much to her credit, calmly echoed back what they said, as if she was on Prozac, and washed it down with "Honey, I'm sorry you're upset, but that's not the way it is." (She never went into detail.) If they persisted with questions about why Dad would have said something like that, she'd throw in, "I don't know, but it isn't so," and then move on to a more pleasant subject like a trip to the mall.

The next time your child tattles on your ex for bad-mouthing you, try one of my mud report lines from the previous page, Carmen's method, or, if your children are older, any of the lines from the Gossip Tolerance Program in chapter 20 (see page 109). Study these applications:

Comment	How You Can Respond
Daddy said you were weird.	Hmmm.
Daddy said he was going to take us from you because you're a drunk.	Well, that's interesting. I might have a word with him about that.
Mommy, is God going to strike you down for divorcing Daddy?	Laugh.

Comment	How You Can Respond
Daddy's wife called you a $@%!!	Hmmm. That wasn't nice, and we don't use that language here. I'll have a word with her about that. (In this instance, use the Pooh-bah Power Talk model on page 92 to do so.)

Never.
1. Show lasting, visible signs of interest or injury.
2. Challenge any drivel your child relays from the other house.

If your child is genuinely upset about Pooh-bah's bad-mouthing you, use the Pooh-bah Power Talk model to discuss it with him in person or by letter, highlighting the benefits of a mudslinging gag order to your child. For example:

"Little Maya was really upset that you said my butt was bigger than the state of Oregon when she was over last weekend. She cried for over an hour after she told me about it, and made herself sick. It would be less traumatizing for her if you didn't mention it again. Thank you."

Your ex will most likely look at you like you said he was a two-headed Sasquatch and deny whatever it was he did or said, but trust me, it cuts down on repeat offenses. And the tattling will dwindle once your children see that the bad words don't ruffle you, and it will also fade when you stop probing, digging, or debriefing them when they return from Dad's. *Capisce?*

Affirmations

1. I free myself from other people's negative visions of me.
2. I love myself and I am a good person.
3. Sticks and stones may break my bones, but names will never hurt me.
4. My good name and good deeds precede me.

27. Spread Out a Little Honey for Your Ex's Honey Too

You know, it probably seems like you and your ex's new wife or semipermanent honey should be natural enemies. Traditionally, as the Queen Bee theory goes, one exalted female per hive, and it's you, right? And, since you've given birth to the "Golden Child" and passed on her new forever love, what's stopping your ex's new honey from bowing to you, sticking "Goddess" before your name when addressing you, and acting like it's a joy and a privilege to know you?

It didn't happen for me that way either, but even though the woman Pooh-bah moved in with shortly after our divorce and married five years later does not kiss my thumb ring, she doesn't give me attitude. She adores him and has a string of pet names to prove it. She adores Esprit too. She's fixed her hair, bought clothes for her, cooked her dinner, laughed with her, and with Pooh-bah's terrible memory, I'm sure she's also the one who reminds him of Esprit's birthday every year.

Does yours come with attitude? Well, make nice with her anyway, because if she's part of his life, she's going to be part of your child's life too. Forty-year-old Rita realized this earlier on when her ex married his 24-year-old assistant and started what she called a "kiss-up" campaign. She invited her for tea, then lunch, then movie nights with her girl-friends, and since they were both trying to lose weight, they started jogging together. "It was work, because I thought she was a twit at first, but I felt that if she got to know me, she'd be kind to my daughter, Stacy, when she was visiting. At the end of a year, I liked her much more than my ex, but I still don't know why she loves that loser." Maybe you won't take the peace party this far, but if you do, God bless you.

Interacting with your ex's new honey can get a little more complicated across the board in any of the following scenarios:

He Is Desecrating You Behind the Scenes

If you think your children are getting an earful about you while they're at their dad's, can you imagine the pillow talk his honey is getting? For all she knows you are the notorious Witch of the Western World. He has, I'm sure, delivered the trumped-up shortcomings of your former love fest with him in Surround Sound. How else would he tell it, and what else would she, the new, improved honey, expect to hear?

One of the biggest mistakes you can make with her during his smear campaign is trying to pit the two of them against each other by telling THE TRUTH and destroying her illusion, so don't bother. Instead, here are six basic commandments that will help you win her over by quietly and subtly proving him wrong from the sidelines:

1. Be cordial or be quiet. (*Note:* If you talk, this is the perfect time to sign her up for Tupperware, magazine subscriptions, candy, and whatever else your child's school is currently peddling. Collect as you go.)
2. Ignore immature, unskillful behavior.
3. Politely refuse to discuss any of your ex's shortcomings, even if the I-want-to-testify-too spirit hits you.
4. Find a feature or personality trait you like about her and genuinely compliment her on it every time you see her (or playact).

5. Apply all techniques throughout the book for Pooh-bah to a Pooh-bah honey.
6. Keep your hands to yourself.

She Is Jealous of Your Continuing Relationship with Him

Why wouldn't she be jealous of you? Although your ex is biting your head off every other time he phones, you're the only other female he talks to and you're getting attention she's not. And, what other former bed partner of his has her phone number and access to her paycheck if Pooh-bah doesn't pay child support? You are also a glaring, ever-present reminder of what can happen if her relationship with Pooh-bah goes sour.

"My ex's wife practically snarls whenever I call to speak to him," says 30-year-old Jessie. "Sometimes she even says he's not home, but I hear the football game in the background. Once I told her I knew he was there, and I really needed to talk to him, and she said she was tired of me always being in *their* lives, and that she would give him the message after the game was over."

The live-in of 25-year-old Morgan's ex doesn't relay messages at all, and every so often she even records an outgoing message on their voice mail that if it's Morgan, she can call Franklin at work. "Sometimes I need to talk to him at home when the kids are with him. It's not fair."

No, it's not fair. Why can't she be mature enough to get over herself, say hello, and pass him the phone? It's not like you really want to talk to him anyway. For that matter, why can't Pooh-bah be more mature? It doesn't matter. You'll drive yourself crazy trying to understand this loony-tunes behavior, so focus instead on taking care of yourself and your child.

As a rule, completely ignore any trifling territorial behavior, and then use playacting or the Pooh-bah Power Talk model (page 92) to get to your goal. Or, if you want to, try this clever statement to help alleviate the honey's anxiety about your being a permanent fixture in her life: "I know this is difficult for you. I'd be a little uncomfortable having another woman call my house to speak to my honey too, but (your ex's name) treasures you. I feel lucky that he's chosen someone so wonderful and moved on with his life. Thank you so much for helping him care for the children."

If you say this in a very genuine, generous, sweet way, with slightly watery eyes, she will be speechless, and hopefully she'll take it as an invitation to be a goddess too.

She Was a Key Factor in Your Breakup

In the movie *She-Devil*, Roseanne Barr spent her days systematically destroying her ex's and his new honey's life after he left her. Fifty-two-year-old Missy lumbered down this road too when her ex divorced her two years ago to move in with his honey of three years. "I thought I was getting even leaving made-up love notes on their car from women I know he'd cheated on me with before her. But since she found out it was me, she's never looked at me the same. She doesn't even say 'hello' now, or have more than two words for my 14-year-old when she's visiting her dad."

They say what goes around comes around, but do you think you've been hired to do the job? The revenge you may be plotting is nowhere near as sweet as getting on to the glorious rest of your life. So, shall we review some of the coping strategies from Part 1 that can help you heal and move from jilted to joy?

Technique	Application
Shower yourself with TLC	Repeat your favorite affirmations, page through your heroes scrapbook, count your blessings, and pamper profusely.
Keep your composure.	Pray, meditate, and playact.
Be your own fairy godmother.	Meditate or journal on the questions on page 33. Add, "How can I spiritualize this?"
Keep things in perspective.	Write a list of 20 things that are just fabulous in your life right now.
Lean on those who love you.	Let your friends and family care for you more right now.

Affirmations

1. My child is loved and well treated by everyone.
2. It is easy for me to have a working relationship with my ex's new wife/love.
3. I'm glad my child has two homes where he is loved and comfortable.

28. Reach Out and Close the Long-Distance Gap

Did Pooh-bah leave town, or did you? You're probably the envy of all your girlfriends who dreamily ask Santa every Christmas to spirit a state or two between them and their exes so they won't have to see them every other Friday. Is the grass really greener on the other side of the country? Maybe it is, maybe it isn't. Let's just say it's different, and that you will have different challenges and opportunities co-parenting cross-country.

For one thing, you have the dreaded task of putting your children on an airplane or train, or packing them up for a long, long drive to dad's house once or twice a year for an extended stay. This is the case for 34-year-old Iowa City resident Cassie, whose 8-year-old daughter, Andrea, spends her two-week winter vacation and eight-week summer vacation with her dad in Philadelphia, and 25-year-old Judy, whose ex drives 20 hours from Aspen to Seattle to retrieve their 4-year-old son every three months for 10 days, according to their parenting agreement.

Also unique to long-distance co-parenting is the separation of your child from familiar faces of friends, community, and the built-in adult support system she or he has locally. "Every summer Josh has to make new friends in his dad's town all over again, and he always misses out on most of the summer with his best friend Brad," says 42-year-old Ashley of her 11-year-old son's summers at his dad's.

And finally, because there's no ongoing every-other-weekend connection when he comes to get your child, and you don't bump into him at sporting events, parent conferences or around town, he may grow to be a virtual stranger, causing unsettling communication gaps.

"The most painful thing I've ever done was put my 7-year-old daughter on a plane to see her dad for the summer. We don't speak much the whole year and then I have to give him our daughter for two months. He's weird about when I can call to speak to her; sometimes my letters to her come back unopened, with a handwritten note on the envelope, 'Return to sender,' and I often have the eerie feeling she's disappeared into a black hole for those two months," says 42-year-old Mikala.

As your children get older, some of your travel anxiety may fade. Kimi, 51, felt much more comfortable about letting her 17-year-old son Miles fly alone from their California home to see his father for two weeks in New York than she did when he was 10. And by that time, one of her brothers—who for reasons unbeknownst to her still liked her ex—relocated to a nearby city and checked in on his nephew regularly.

Long-distance visitation is an intriguing opportunity for your children, albeit somewhat disjointed and anxiety-ridden for you, but if you work at it, it can work for you. Here's a seven-week campaign to help you close the gap between you and your ex and you and your children while they're away.

Week 1: Review your "Me" list in Part 1 (page 21) and intensify your efforts around the goals specific to long-distance parenting.

Week 2: Make a list of concerns you have and use the Pooh-bah Power Talk model on page 92 to discuss the top three with your ex after you confirm visitation dates. This model can also be used to smooth over any problems that arise while your children are away.

Week 3: Contact anyone you know in the area who can

check in with your children for local support and up-dates.

Week 4: Talk to your children about their upcoming visit, outlining their stay, telling them how you will miss them, and how happy you are that they're going to spend time with Dad. Then answer any questions they have.

Week 5: Prepare a care package for your children which may include: a letter or series of letters they can read while they are away (or taped "talking" letters for smaller children); a favorite storybook or CD; a piece of your jewelry, a small throw, or something they can wear or snuggle with that reminds them of you; for teens, emergency numbers in case they have one and cannot reach you.

Week 6: Develop a contact schedule. Will you send a letter once a week, call every fourth day to chat for a few minutes, etc.? Also encourage your children's friends and relatives to write to them.

Week 7: Spend special time with your children.

Day of departure: Do the send-off ritual (#3 below).

Affirmations

1. My child is always safe and loved.
2. I am glad my child can travel to spend time with her father.
3. I remain lovingly connected to my child wherever he is.

Ritual #3

This is a three-part ritual, and you will design the first two parts because they will be based on the spirit of your relationship with your child. Once you customize it by plugging in activities from your day-to-day routine, perform the entire ritual whenever your child goes off to visit his dad.

1. A pre-handoff activity

Do something that makes you feel extra close to your child, such as:

- Preparing a favorite meal
- Playing a favorite game or movie
- Sharing a pampering ritual
- Reciting a prayer or story
- Exercising together
- Performing a song or dance

2. A loving good-bye

Send your child off in an endearing way:

- Create a unique salute or a secret handshake
- Place a piece of your jewelry or a token about her
- Give her a special hug
- Recite a rhyme or a call-and-response script

3. A visualization

When your children leave, do the following visualization:

Sit quietly for a few minutes with a photo of your children pressed to your heart. Image clearly their smile, their laughter, their physical well-being, and their safe return to you.

꽃

It's time for a pampering break! Before you continue on, treat yourself to something from your master pampering list.

꽃

❧ PART 4 ❧

Money

Most of my first child support payments were late or short and they often looked more like ransom money than child support payments. Why he preferred to give me a wad of smoky, wrinkled, crumpled bills over a crisp check I'll never know. Nor will I know why he insisted on relinquishing his hold on it only after carefully scrutinizing my face, as if he were expecting me to break down and confess to secretly planning to take a trip to Aruba with the $300 he'd just pressed into my hand. On one occasion, he counted it out in front of me, meditatively, as if he were paying the tax on his soul. Knowing he'd just as soon burn the money as give it to me, I started to bless it. And soon after that, I began putting together other coping strategies to ease me through this wildly aggravating dimension of our new relationship.

29. Make Sure You Have a Child Support Order

One Monday morning, in the midst of their epic 14-month-long divorce proceedings, 49-year-old Glady's ex stood in the courtroom in front of her, her attorney, the judge, and God, charging that he should not be liable for child support, because they had never consummated their marriage. Ten years, no sex, so how could he possibly be the father of "her" 7-year-old daughter?

"While my attorney and I faced each other stunned, the judge quietly beckoned him to her bench with a measured finger wiggle. Then she leaned down, never taking her eyes off him, apparently studying him for evidence of head trauma, and said, 'Mr. Blank, I'm going to move on to the next case on my docket, so you can rethink this. Do you understand? We'll call you back in within the half hour.'

"Twenty minutes later, he recited the same lie, without a stutter. Shaking her head, she ordered a paternity test for his daughter, who looks just like him, whom he's raised for seven years, and he's now paying $500 a month."

Sad to say, aerobic child support avoidance stories like this one abound, and they can often deter many women from pursuing a child support order, as do these generic turnoffs: (1) It's another living, breathing entity between the two of you. (2) You find yourself knowing you'll have to put "don't know" in too many of those spots regarding his income and whereabouts. (3) You know he's going to squabble over every line. (4) You know he doesn't have two pennies to rub together. (5) You know he's going to be a pain in the butt to collect from anyway, so why bother. (6) It's too much paperwork.

I promise you, as a longtime form-phobe, if I'd been in the money when I looked at that child support worksheet for the first time, I'd have sloughed it off indefinitely. And I would have been dead wrong—money bags or not—because two people are financially responsible for raising a child, unless, of course, you really are the Virgin Mary. So, if you haven't already, finalize your child support order. It will help do three things:

1. Clearly define your joint financial responsibility toward your child (basic living expenses, day care, medical care, special child-rearing expenses, etc.).
2. Establish a period of financial responsibility.
3. Set forth terms of payment (e.g., through a state registry payroll deduction, alternative arrangement, or directly to the residential parent).

Affirmations

1. I am willing to make sure my child's needs are met.
2. I easily complete tedious financial paperwork.

30. Rise Above the At-ti-tude That Comes with the Money

Wouldn't it be splendid if your ex handed you child support and said, "Thank you so much for taking such excellent care of our child? Do you need anything else?" If you're like most women with a difficult ex, not only have you never heard anything remotely close to this, but you've also witnessed him doing and saying things that leave you with the feeling that instead of giving the money to you, he would rather burn it, donate it to Ethiopian refugees, buy a new sports car or hair transplant, pay back taxes to the IRS, or rough himself up, stagger into the police station the day before it's due, and file a mugging report.

Do any of these sound familiar?

- *Yolanda, 39:* "The check usually has a slightly damp residue. I get the feeling it's spit."
- *Rosie, 26:* "When my son Mitch needed braces and I asked my ex to pay half, he blamed me for not taking better care of him. Like I'd fed him something to make his teeth crooked?"
- *Samantha, 33:* "According to him, he's the only one making sacrifices to provide for the kids. When I asked him for a mangy $25 last week to buy soccer cleats for Jamie, he said, 'There goes my beer again.' "
- *Donnie, 26:* "He tapes the child support check to the inside of our daughter's coat, after having her memorize his your-mother's-bleeding-me-dry sermon."
- *Becky, 42:* "My ex is the original bean counter, and he

thinks he's my budget advisor now. He has the nerve to ask me where I shop for basics and to offer ideas for shopping more frugally. How far does he think $400 goes?"

Coping with Attitude

Melinda found her ex's wounded-wallet routine decreased when she set up direct deposit into her checking account through her local child support registry. "I think because the money comes straight out of his check, he doesn't immediately miss it enough to get himself all worked up anymore."

If most of your Pooh-bah's groaning usually occurs with hand-to-hand child support transfers, and another dissertation about the hardship you've caused in his life makes you want to put one hand on either side of his head and see if it will spin around like Linda Blair's did in *The Exorcist*, request a direct deposit as Melinda did. Or you can arrange to have him mail it to you, pay it to a third party, or make lump-sum payments (quarterly, semiannually, or yearly).

His Meddling Fan Club

Pooh-bah's not the only whiner in the bunch, so you might also get labeled as the arch villain by his admiring friends, family, honey, and assorted busybodies who've rallied over to the child-support-should-be-optional camp and obviously know way too much of your business.

I was giving a former childless friend a ride home one day, and she noticed the pile of Department of Child Support (DCS) paperwork in my backseat. We had a brief conversation that went something like this:

Her: Why are you going to turn him in to DCS?

Me: Because he's reneging on his financial pledge to Esprit, and I'm tired of stalking him on his paydays.

Her: Well, he just got married, didn't he? They're probably still paying for the wedding. Why don't you give him a few more months?

Me: Did your father take care of you when you were little?

Her: Yes.

Me: What would you have expected your mother to have done if he hadn't?

She didn't answer. Maybe because she was in *my* car and I was glaring at her like I'd just figured out she was part of a special experimental lobotomy follow-up group. We were also a good six-hour freeway hike from the city. But she still had that I know-I'm-hosed-if-I-answer-truthfully-but-I-still-think-I'm-right look on her face.

Some of your ex's people might even drop out of your life before you kick them out. "Ken's [her ex] mother had the unmitigated gall to call and scold me a day before the kids were to visit them because I'd filed a contempt suit against their doctor son who hasn't paid his $600-a-month child support for over five months. She ended the call with, 'Tell the children they can come again when you leave our boy alone,' " recalled 39-year-old Emmy.

Anyone who questions your right to child support has had one too many contact highs from topping off at the gas pump. Distraction and direct dismissal—if you no longer want these snakes in your life now that you know where they slither—will work quite nicely.

Affirmations

1. Money comes to me easily and joyfully.
2. My child deserves to have financial support, and I forgive everyone who doesn't yet see this.

31. Collect Your Child Support

If Sigmund Freud were still alive, I'm sure he would have some interesting things to say about the nature of the dead-beat parent syndrome. When my ex and I were still married, we theorized about it too and jointly agreed that, psychobabble aside, there were only two reasons dead-beats don't pay child support: (1) They don't have the money. (2) They don't want to. So, first things first, let's figure out which group your ex falls into, and then, if it's the latter, I'll help you put together a collection strategy. Now, pick your ex out of the following lineup:

#1—Mr. Lay Z. Bum

Standard traits: Frequently unemployed, underemployed, or job-hopper; regards unemployment as an acceptable form of ongoing income. AMBITIONS: To win the Publisher's Clearinghouse sweepstakes and loaf around for the rest of his Earth days. FAVORITE PUBLICATION: *TV Guide.* FAVORITE PLACE: the couch. PASTIMES: sleeping, thinking about sleeping, and being annoyed at anything that interferes with sleep.

Collection potential: Nil. You're way too affirmation-happy if you think you're going to shake money out of an empty piggy bank. You'll have to make your own money. Go directly to Chapter 36.

#2—Mr. Hyde the Money

Standard traits: Works for cash, works under assumed names, may have more than one Social Security number and ID card, changes jobs almost as frequently as Mr. Lay Z. Bum, has no traceable employer of record, yet he's driving a fancier car than you are. AMBITIONS: To become Mr. Deadbeat Dad of the Year by hiding as many assets as possible while living a lavish life. FAVORITE PUBLICATION: Underground hide-the-money-type publications mailed in brown bags. FAVORITE PLACE: Entrepreneur expos, secretive, member-only deadbeat dad retreats, and home seminars on hiding money. PASTIMES: Attending entrepreneur expos, getting a new fake ID made, publicly whining about not having any money while wearing his Italian-made ensemble.

Collection potential: Fair, but you have to slip on your detective hat and keep tabs on him. See Collection Strategy #1 below and Collection Strategy #3 in Chapter 33.

#3—Mr. E. Z. Collect

Standard traits: Legitimately employed blue-collar, professional, military, or high-profile career man with a strong work ethic; filled out W-4 form, using correct Social Security number; gets paid on a regular basis by an above-board company; owns and wears a company T-shirt. AMBITIONS: To be employee of the year; to become his boss's boss. FAVORITE PUBLICATIONS: *Inc.,* the *Wall Street Journal* or industry trade magazines. FAVORITE PLACE: Work. PASTIMES: Networking, career advancement seminars, kissing up to his boss, attending company picnics.

Collection potential: High. His job is his world. He may not want to give you the money willingly, but if he receives a regular paycheck and his employer is participating in a child support registry as required by law in most states, you can have his check garnisheed. See Collection Strategy #2 and Collection Strategy #3 (in Chapter 33).

Collection Strategy #1

1. Gather information about his covert earnings—business licenses and location, income, clients, and employees—from the Small Business Administration, friendly spies, and gossipy people. I collected 80 percent of such information in casual conversation with my ex's associates by pretending I was overjoyed that he was Mr. Entrepreneur. For some reason, I mysteriously kept bumping into people who knew both of us while we were married, who had heard he'd started this-or-that business, and they wanted to know if I had his number. Nose around.
2. Have Power Talks and stress motivating negative consequences if he does not comply (see Collection Strategy #3).
3. Get someone else to enforce your support order (see Collection Strategy #3).

Collection Strategy #2

1. Place reminder calls.
2. Provide pickup service.
3. Have Power Talks and stress motivating benefits and negative consequences if he does not comply (see Collection Strategy #3).
4. Get someone else to enforce your support order (see Collection Strategy #3).

Money Power Talks

Journey when you have to, and then keep pointing out benefits, and requesting the money, or getting him to agree to a future payment date. Here are a few excuses for not paying child support I've heard over the years that I feel should qualify for public flogging should it ever gain acceptance again:

- I forgot.
- My new computer cost more than I thought, so I'm a little short this month.
- I left the child support money in the freezer and my roommate's friend stole it.
- My paycheck was short, and I thought I didn't have to pay if I didn't get a full check.
- I didn't have time to get to the bank. Would you take me?
- How much was I supposed to give you again?
- Esprit's in Mexico for the summer, and I didn't think I had to pay when she was abroad.
- I only have cash now and I'd like to get a money order, so can it wait until next week?
- The IRS garnisheed my check. Those bums.

Don't let anger, disgust, or dismay distract you from your goal. *Get the money.* Here is a focused Money Power Talk from my archives.

THE MONEY POWER TALK

I Forgot/I Haven't Cashed My Check

On this particular day, he was over a week late with child support, and since he'd ignored three requests for a return phone call, I paid a surprise visit to him at his job.

Objective: To get the money.

15 Minutes Prior to the Visit

To center myself, I sat in my car practicing the Happy Count, visualizing myself on a Caribbean beach and Pooh-bah jogging by momentarily to hand me the child support money with a smile.

The Visit

Fortunately, he worked at a neighboring business and the receptionist had seen me drop off Esprit before, so she let me in without warning him. I walked over to his cubicle and began the following conversation:

Me, starting with warm-up chitchat and ending with my request: Well, hi there! You are okay. I was worried when you didn't call me back. Glad to see you're all right. *(I sat down in a neighboring swivel chair and rolled it over beside him and complimented the artwork he had on his desk.)* Yada, yada, yada . . . Listen, I'm here to pick up child support.

Pooh-bah: It's that time again? I forgot. I haven't cashed my check yet. Can I get it to you tomorrow?

(I began to daydream about tracking down my college sweetheart, whom I suddenly regretted not having married instead of Pooh-bah.)

Me, pointing out the benefits of giving me the money today: No, today's best. I have to get Esprit's basketball shoes later. *(This was an absolute lie since I'd bought her shoes the day before.)* Could you make a run to your bank now?

Pooh-bah: I can't leave work. I've got to get this job done.

Me (holding out my hand and noting curiously that the guy in the adjacent cube had gotten church-mouse quiet and might even be holding his breath so he could eavesdrop): Okay, I'll take an installment for now then, and I'll be by to get the rest tomorrow morning.

Pooh-bah (ushers me out to the hallway, turns his pockets inside out, plunks $150 worth of $5's, $10's, and $20's into

*my hand, and gives me his will-you-please-leave-now?
shrug):* That's all I have. Now I won't even have lunch
money.
Me, reminding him of my next-day return: "Okay, this will
cover today. Thank you. I'll get Esprit's shoes. And then I'll
be back tomorrow for the rest, around this same time,
okay?"
Pooh-bah: Okay, I'll be here.

Note: If you have a Power Money Talk over the phone, make
sure you make use of that mute button if you have to gag or
feel a few unmentionables coming on, and pamper yourself
afterwards.

Affirmations

1. I am diligent and resourceful about collecting child
   support.
2. Communicating about money comes easy to me.

32. MIND YOUR MONEY

Now, for a little not-so-good news. After all of your industrious collection efforts, it may still take a while to get the money. It's also possible that Pooh-bah may not pay at all, and even if he does, it may not be enough for you to afford the style of living you're used to. Shall we commiserate, or shall we strategize?

The Economic Mindfulness Strategy

For a lot of people, budgeting is synonymous with enormous mortal suffering. It can bring on a slew of unpleasant emotions similar to those that accompany cramps—pain, rage, and tears—and scant visions of bread, Spam, and water. So we're not going to talk about budgeting. Economic mindfulness, on the other hand, is a creative expression of the spirit that enables you to make conscientious spending choices and make more of what you already have.

Step 1: Give It a Number

I know you've been practicing your first-response insights to come up with ideas to get along with Pooh-bah, but now I want you to turn them inward again, and use them to come up with a very special number. Close your eyes and, breathing in a very relaxed manner, take a moment to consider your basic monthly expenses—shelter, food, transportation, day care, bills and other standard expenses, your child's needs, entertainment, and emergency funds. Let your mind wander past the traditional thoughts about what you should have to what you want to have, and make sure you throw in a few dollars for pampering. And without turning it over in your mind too many times, write a dollar amount in the left margin of this page. *The first figure that comes to mind is correct.* We're going to work with that number in much more detail in Chapter 36. Right now, we'll focus on ways to trick your mind into believing you have that amount until you get it.

Step 2: Simplify Your Life

Reduce or release all expensive or compulsive habits, such as drinking, smoking, shopping, and owning the latest-and-greatest of anything. Cut up your credit cards, cancel frivolous subscriptions and memberships, and commit to bringing select things into your life that you truly enjoy and are within your means.

Step 3: Look for Bargains

There are free lunches. Free dinners too. My church hosts one once a month. The library has free books, tapes, and videos for you to borrow on every subject from aromatherapy to Zen meditation. City parks, beaches, and forests are free too. Take a hike, hug a tree, swim the lake. Supermarkets also have many bargains. Clip coupons and become the buy-one-get-one-free queen. And, if there's something you want for yourself or your children and you can't get it free, then look around for an opportunity to get it at a reduced price. Did you know that you can get student rates for services at many massage, acupuncture, dental, and beauty schools? Request a soon-to-graduate student, and offer up your body.

Step 4: Make Less Seem Like More

When I'm absolutely broke, you can find me in the kitchen gathering remnants from my cupboards and refrigerator to whip up an elegant gourmet meal. The table is set with purple napkins, of course, and candles, with some happy-time CD playing in the background. Since I've learned to cook all of our favorite restaurant meals and ethnic delights (Thai, Mexican, Chinese, Indian) on a barebones budget, I can produce two plates that look as if they're straight out of the pages of *Bon Appétit* or *Saveur* (which I study often and earnestly). I'm also not beyond breaking out the chopsticks or sombrero, or popping on a suitable matching CD to top off my ethnic-theme dinners. Even a Waldorf salad and steamed brown rice with a twig of parsley and a slice of lemon make me feel like I have a few gold bars in my safety-deposit box. In addition to creative gourmet meals, Esprit and I have treasure hunts, name-that-tune-a-thons, storytelling nights, fireside chats, dance contests, and two-person plays in our apartment all the time.

Step 5: Accept Charity

"My dad was over for dinner one night. Afterward, he played with my boys and tucked them in. Then he came back into the living room, kissed me good night, and told me I was a wonderful mother, and not to let anything my ex, Austin, said make me believe otherwise. Later, when I went to pull the covers up over the boys, I noticed an envelope taped to their dresser mirror with my name written on it. It was a check for $2,000. It said, 'Consider this an early Mother's Day gift. And do not spend it all on the boys. I love you. Dad. P.S. If you don't cash it in five days, I will return with cash, and if you ever mention it to me, I'll deny it,' " shared 31-year-old Kaitlin.

Remember the support team you identified in Chapter 11 (page 69)? If you've squeezed every dime in the house and you're at risk of being homeless or having a baby heart attack, call one of them and ask for a sanity grant or loan. And express gratitude for whatever form the occasional unexpected sanity loan or love gift comes in.

Step 6: Create a Bill-Paying Strategy

If you are behind in your payments, contact your creditors to set up payment plans based on what you have available. If they are unwilling to oblige, contact your local Consumer Credit Counseling Service (CCCS) office for assistance. CCCS counselors are trained to intercede with your creditors on your behalf, at very low cost. "I put all of my bills in a shoebox and carted them down to a counselor at Consumer Credit Counseling Service, and said, 'Please do something with this.' After one hour, she told me she'd set up a payment plan with my creditors and I'd have everything paid off in three years, and that's just fine with me," says 42-year-old Alana. Here are some other do-and-don't bill-paying strategies from single moms.

- Do have a positive attitude when you're paying creditors. "My creditors are not the enemy, and I want to pay them back. So even when things are tight, I pay what I can, and I write little smiley faces on my check."—*Suzanne, 25*
- Do respond to collection inquiries. "Why hide from them? I want to teach my children to be responsible for their debts, so I return the when-are-we-going-to-get-our-money? calls, even if it's just to tell them, 'No time soon, I'm sorry.' "—*Bonita, 42*
- Don't spend all of your money paying bills. "I contacted my creditors to let them know I was having money problems, but I still wanted to keep my credit

clean. Then I bought $200 worth of $10 money orders (10 percent of what I make) and mailed them out."
—Cyndi, 34

• Don't pay your bills until you have the money in your hand. "If your ex is late with child support most of the time, and you count on that money to pay bills, save yourself some embarrassment by waiting until it's in your hands before you write a check against it."
—Dina, 36

Step 7: Create an Emergency Account

You're never as strapped as you think you are, especially if you tuck something away in advance for a rainy day. Most financial advisors suggest two to three months of income in a separate emergency account that will tide you over to your next sunny day. Many banks will let you open an account with as little as $50, so start building your emergency fund today from whatever you have. How can you pad your emergency account?

1. Liquidate excess or undesirable assets, such as art, real estate, clothing, furniture, vehicles, books, electronic equipment, CDs, and anything else you are reducing in step 2 (page 162).

2. Earmark all windfalls, bonuses, investments, money gifts, tax refunds, and raises for your emergency fund until you have three months' worth tucked away. Also, until you hit the three-month mark, when someone asks you if you need anything, say $50 and plunk it into your account.

3. Manifest more abundance in your life. See Chapter 36.

Step 8: Set up a Joy Account

While you're being frugal, if you have to, you can still flavor your life. In fact, I believe it's essential that you do so right now. Create a joy account to go along with your emergency account, and keep a minimum of what it will cost to get your very favorite pampering item in it at all times. Withdraw from it as needed to get your monthly dose of pampering. Copy your master pampering list (see pages 45–47) and give it to the people who regularly buy you birthday, holiday, and special occasion gifts.

Step 9: Save 10 Percent of What You Earn

Every time you get money, put 10 percent of it into a savings or investment account. Like your emergency account, this will create another nest egg that will put you one step closer to your financial dynasty. If you work for someone else, check into having that amount directly deducted from your paycheck and rolled into something like a 401K.

Step 10: Give Something Back

Once, when we were approaching the tithing portion of a church service, my minister, who usually doesn't really make a big deal out of the whole thing, said, "Every time you give, it comes back to you. But that's not the only reason to give. Give because you can, even if it's a quarter, because it lets the universe know that you are investing in something other than yourself. And when you give, give with joy, or it's worthless. If you give like a miser, or from a place of lack and scarcity, your money loses its value. So, if you don't feel happy about what you're going to put in the basket today, please keep it."

You can tithe money at church, give to the Girl Scouts, buy something your child is peddling for school, adopt a family to buy Christmas presents for, or volunteer your time or expertise. When you do, whatever it is, make sure you do it with a joyful spirit, knowing that you are abundantly blessed, and you really do have it to give.

Affirmations

1. Through my rich spirit, I create a rich life.
2. I can be relaxed and happy while obtaining the income I desire.
3. I give and receive in the same loving spirit.

33. If You Have to, Get Someone Else to Enforce Your Child Support Order

Perhaps you've already earned an honorary "life-experience" doctorate in collections while trying to squeeze child support out of your ex, and you're more than a little burnt out from trying to get a grown man to take care of his child. If you've got either a Mr. Hyde the Money or a Mr. E. Z. Collect, and over the past six months you can answer yes to at least three of the statements below, you've graduated to Collection Strategy #3.

Yes **No**

____ ____ 1. Reminded him of his past-due child support payment more times than you reminded your child to brush her teeth or bathe.

____ ____ 2. Stalked him at his job, home, or bank on paydays.

____ ____ 3. Heard one too many lame excuses, like "The dog ate the money," about why he can't pay.

____ ____ 4. Spied him spending frivolously on other things (like that new Ferrari).

____ ____ 5. Taken to rationing paper towels.

____ ____ 6. Graciously handed your child over to him for visitation even though he was behind in child support, and then heard enough delirious Daddy-got-me-this-and-Daddy-

Yes   No   got-me-that reports from your returning
                    junk food–stuffed child to convince you
                    that he spent at least half of the child sup-
                    port on entertaining her.

____ ____   7. Seen his picture in the local business
                    paper under "Promotions," or "Up and
                    Coming" the day after he told you he
                    was laid off.

____ ____   8. Have been labeled "slow pay" by your
                    creditors, because your ex is a slow pay.

____ ____   9. Have been frequently forced into vegetar-
                    ianism, although a devout carnivore.

____ ____   10. Turned scrounging for couch and car seat
                    change into a pastime.

Collection Strategy #3

1. Put together a log of his payments and information
   about his employer, address, Social Security number,
   business licenses and clients, and suspected covert
   earnings.

2. If you have $150 or more to spend on hourly legal
   fees, contact an attorney who specializes in divorce or
   family law. If not, call your local Division of Child
   Support Services (DCS) to request a copy of the paperwork to open a case with them.

3. If you go with an attorney, schedule an informational
   appointment, present your paperwork, and he or she
   will take it from there. If you go the DCS route,
   they're going to send you a fat pack of forms that may
   bring on a huge spell of brain sore, so plan lots of
   pampering.

Division of Child Support Services (DCS) or Private Attorney?

	Advantages	**Disadvantages**
DCS	• FREE • Good odds of collecting from Mr. E. Z. Collect	• Pokey-butt slow • High client-to-caseworker ratio
Private attorney	• Potentially swift collection • Fairly low client to attorney ratio	• Costly • May not yield anything

All in all, my collection efforts consistently netted more in five years than the four payments DCS garnisheed out of Pooh-bah's paychecks before he left that job. All of this money drama has seeped into my subconscious. One night, I had a dream that I'd been interrogating a tied-up Pooh-bah in a dingy basement using Chinese water torture. After what seemed like days, he still hadn't agreed to turn over any money, and I was moving on to shock treatments when suddenly the police burst in, cornered me, and carted me off to a psych unit. I was screaming, "I know he's got the money! Why are you taking *me* away?!"

It may take a little bit more time to get child support again, but because I went through the DCS system, if Pooh-bah ever works for a legitimate employer again and gives his real name and Social Security number on his W-4, they will be required to notify DCS, who will then move to garnishee his wages.

Affirmations

1. I am persistently in pursuit of my desires.
2. The more I have to do in the world, the more my self-care routines increase.

34. Share Your Child Even When You Don't Get Child Support

Whenever you set a grace goal for yourself, you will always be tested on it very quickly, in the biggest way possible. When I was about two pages into Part 4, Pooh-bah stopped paying child support. But did he stop showing up to whisk Esprit away for fun-filled weekends? No. And did he have the nerve to flame-call me for reporting him to my new friend at the Division of Child Support Services for default? Yes.

Believe you me, my first thoughts when he came to the door that second or third month of not paying were *not* "Oh joy! It's Pooh-bah come to spend time with Esprit." You should probably also know that I was between jobs, had to cash out my IRA to take care of bills, health insurance, etc., and was very close to becoming a reluctant vegetarian again.

Three thoughts kept recurring in my heckler mind whenever Mr. Hyde the Money called or showed up at my front door for Esprit:

1. Was caning an acceptable resolution for default of child support? And, if not, could I get off on the crime-of-passion plea bargain?
2. Would I be arrested for littering if I posted flyers with his picture on every lamppost in the city that said: "Child Support Avoider. Do not sell or buy anything from this man, because he has not paid child support FOR A WHOLE YEAR"?

3. Could I be slapped with a mail-solicitation fine for sending out envelopes for donations to his friends and relatives similar to the ones charities mail out to gather donations for the holidays? And would something like "Please help Nailah set the Thanksgiving table for Esprit" sound too pathetic?

Fortunately, the heckler has always been very concerned about Esprit's mental health and also does not want to see me in ankle cuffs, so she "journeyed" through those pickups.

Thirty-two-year-old Spring says, "I booked my son Jason up for months to teach his nonpaying dad a lesson. I don't even know why he kept calling to see him. I would have been ashamed. He threatened to take me to court for contempt of visitation, and I just kept scheduling, looking forward, in a sick way, to court. If he had the money to take me to court, why wasn't he paying his child support? But Jason started acting up in school, and I knew it was because he missed his dad, whom he loves, so I stopped hiding him out."

Your kids still want to see their fathers, so mentally separate visitation from child support, by playacting, if you have to, to get through visitation pickups and drop-offs.

Affirmations

1. I am willing to share my child with her father.
2. Every day, I find it easier to separate my child's visits to her father from child support.
3. I see the ultimate good in my child spending time with her dad.

35. Persist with Collections Until the Check Is in the Bank

If you still haven't gotten your child support and you've tried Collection Strategies #1, #2, and #3, here's a final ray of hope—primarily for Mr. Hyde the Money—that has recently yielded interesting developments for me.

The idea for it came while I was reading the day's mail on a stationary bike one December afternoon. In the pile was a postcard from my mayor, complete with a report card of his accomplishments while in office. A fine man, I thought, doing good things for the community and our families. Then, just like that, I made a mental note to contact him when I got home to see if he might help me collect child support. During the 30-minute drive home—via the winery to pick up a bottle of my favorite wine to toast another finished chapter of my book—the target of my letter escalated from the mayor to the president. Luckily, by the time I finally sat down at the computer with my wine beside me, I'd downgraded to my state senators. I'd get a quicker reply from them anyway, I thought, since Bill was so busy with the impeachment and all. I took a sip and typed the following letter to both of my senators. *(Note: All identifying contact information has been changed to protect the privacy of all involved.)*

December 8, 1998
Re: Collecting Child Support Arrears and Modification

Dear Senators,

My ex-husband stopped paying child support a little over a year ago, and I referred the matter to the Division of Child Support (DCS). They were able to garnishee his wages for a few months, but he is no longer with that company.

I don't know where he's working now, or if he's working, although it does seem a little unusual that the average person could be unemployed for a whole year and not be homeless.

The other related issue is that I put in for a child support modification this summer. For the past six years, it has been $###.##, and this amount no longer represents our daughter's financial needs. DCS reviewed my paperwork and told me a few weeks ago that they wouldn't be able to proceed since he has no reported income.

I know DCS is doing the best they can under the circumstances, but a year is more than enough time to bring this issue to a close. I now need more R-E-S-O-U-R-C-E-S so I can collect arrears and be granted a modification.

To top it all off, I was laid off in July and I am still unemployed. I am living on my savings and my imagination. My daughter should not have to. Can you help me see that she is financially supported by both of her parents?

Thanks in advance for any assistance you can provide, and happy holidays,

Nailah Shami

On the eve of my thirty-eighth birthday, after a multitude of handoffs of Esprit to Pooh-bah, I received three incredible "gifts" in response to my letter:

1. February 26, 1999—a letter from Senator Slade Gorton:

Dear Ms. Shami,

Thank you for your letter regarding your concerns with DCS. I appreciate your bringing this matter to my attention.

I have contacted DCS on your behalf, and asked them to report back to my office. When I have received a reply, I will notify you.

If you have any questions or if you would like further assistance please contact John T. Enforcer in my Bellevue office.

Sincerely,

SLADE GORTON
United States Senator

2. March 8, 1999—a call from a Community Relations specialist at DCS headquarters. He said Slade Gorton's office called, and DCS has referred my case to the prosecuting attorney, and on pain of jail, Pooh-bah will be forced to produce his income records so they can help me collect arrears and current support and process my child support modification.
3. March 8, 1999—a letter from the Director of Washington State's Division of Child Support.

Dear Ms. Shami,

Thank you for your recent letter to Senator Slade Gorton. He asked me, as Director of Washington State's Division of Child Support (DCS), to respond to your concerns. I am sorry that DCS has been unable to collect child support from Pooh-bah. It is difficult to collect child support when a person changes jobs frequently, works for cash, or is self-employed. Your Support Enforcement Officer has referred your case to the King County Prosecutor for contempt action. It will take a while to set up a contempt case, so I encourage you not to expect results immediately. However, Pooh-bah will be called to task by Superior Court for not paying his child support and he will be required to produce his income records. Once DCS receives his income records, we may be able to pursue a modification more effectively.

Again, thank you for bringing your case to my attention. I hope that my comments help to bring some of your concerns to resolution.

Sincerely,

Maya Angel, Director
Division of Child Support

I don't know how it will all go, but at least the wheels of justice are rolling again, and I deeply thank all of my child support intervention team for that. And, although I generally vote Democrat, and Slade Gorton is a Republican, he has my vote if he runs again, for anything.

I said all of this to say, *Get your child's child support.* If I had a middle name, the new love of my life often teases that it would be "Relentless." Make sure you are too. If I went above and beyond for five years with reminder calls, Money Power Talks, and payment pickup service, so can you. If I got beyond my debilitating form-phobia to fill out voluminous mounds of child support collection paperwork, while still handing Esprit off to him for visits, so can you. If I could get collection help from my senator, so can you. What, you say, it's because I'm a somebody? Well, keep in mind that although I've been in newspapers in connection with the annual NGAWYEM campaign—my 10 seconds of fame—Senator Gorton probably didn't recognize my name any more than your senators will yours. So try this at home. It may take a lot of paperwork, ingenuity, prayer, and pampering, but don't you dare forfeit your child's financial birthright.

Affirmations

1. I am willing to let others help me secure justice.
2. Creativity and resourcefulness spill over into everything I do.

36. Manifest More Abundance in Your Life

"There is no reason why dreams should dry up like raisins. . . . I believe that we can impose beauty on our future."
—Lorraine Hansberry

Tired of scrounging around for couch and car change; cursing Pooh-bah in your Small Thoughts journal for your financial woes; playing eenie-meenie-miney-moe with your bills; and waiting for justice to make its way to your bank account? Are you ready to start creating more abundance in your life today?

Good. I've already gone over some ways you can embellish what you have on hand now, but it's time to take another step. It's time to create an abundant mind, which will help you draw more money into your life, so you can come face-to-face with the figure you wrote in step 1 of the Economic Mindfulness Strategy on page 160, or more.

First, I want you to take the biggest bill you have ($50 or more) or a magazine clipping of a big bill, place it on your altar, and allow it to remain there for at least 90 days. I want you to do this right now, so if you have neither a large bill nor a picture of one, then write yourself a deposit slip for the amount you desire. Or better yet, since nothing says abundance like really big money, make the deposit slip out for $1,000,000.00 (break the cash and checks down into any denominations you like) and leave it undated. If you sit before a huge deposit slip every night for the next 90 days, even a pretend deposit slip, especially one for $1,000,000, I guarantee you will quickly develop an abundant mind.

Next, go to the library and check out three books from the moneymaking or entrepreneur section of the library.

You're going to use them a little later, so make sure you find books that appeal to you and have catchy titles like *Making Money from Home, 100 Ways to Make Big Money,* or *Moneymaking Moms: How Work at Home Can Work for You* (this one is a real title by Caroline Hull and Tanya Wallace). When you've got your books in hand, meet me in the next section with a pad of paper.

Your Prosperity Think-athon

This prosperity think-athon will grow your abundant mind even more. First, write down your monthly money goal, the figure in the margin on page 161. Then subtract your present income from it. The figure you have left is your extra money goal. Now, I want you to let your mind flow wild as you answer the questions that follow, until you have at least 20 answers each for 1, 2, and 4, and ten answers for 3 and 5. *Do not put your pen down until you are finished.*

1. What activities do I enjoy?
2. What am I good at, or what could I be good at, that someone would pay me to do?
3. What are my lifelong dreams?
4. What are other people I know doing for extra money? (Use your three library books if you run out of ideas for this one.)
5. What can I do to make extra money?

When you're done, you should have gobs of moneymaking ideas that you can do while having some fun. Perhaps you can enlist your child and work toward a lifelong dream. Go ahead and circle at least two moneymaking possibilities that you're most excited about, and use one of your moneymaking library books to start designing your abundance plan. Here's an example:

Elisha, 36, Teacher

Extra Money Goal: $500 more a month.

1. *What activities do I enjoy?* Reading, knitting, singing, dominoes, skating, softball, movies, Tai chi, sewing and clothes design, dancing, Internet-surfing, going to the park with my sons, styling hair, gift-wrapping, cooking French food, flower arrangement, photography, catalog shopping, organizing, pottery, journaling, playing with my dog, party planning, cake decorating.

2. *What am I good at, or what could I be good at, that someone would pay me to do?* Typing, tax preparation, cleaning, teaching French, teaching tennis, researching, babysitting, dog sitting, landscaping, organizing, salsa dancing, sewing and alterations, preparing gift baskets, interior design, shooting family portraits, modeling, errand running, hairstyling, hosting home jewelry parties, decorating cakes, sales, driving, fashion consulting, massage, singing.

3. *What are my lifelong dreams?* To travel the world, to know I was a good mom, to design a clothing line, to write an award-winning song, to be independently wealthy, to own a home in France, to win a salsa dancing competition, to get a Ph.D. in French literature, to send my sons to college, to sky dive at least once.

4. *What are other people I know doing for extra money?* Renting out part of their house, consigning clothes, playing the stock market, hosting foreign exchange students, planning weddings, catering, singing at a local nightclub on the weekends, travel agent, selling Mary Kay, selling scrapbooks, house-sitting, reselling antiques they buy at secondhand stores, delivering pizza, telemarketing, painting houses, hauling, teaching aerobics, publishing a parenting newsletter, bookkeeping, psychic readings.

5. *What can I do to make extra money?* Host French exchange students, offer French-theme catered meals to
   corporations, get a booth at a flea market and sell
   some of my pottery, take family portraits, start a fashion consulting/design business, teach crash courses in
   French to travelers, freelance photography for magazines, offer salsa lessons, start a gift-wrapping service,
   publish a French culture newsletter.

Affirmations

1. I enjoy creating abundance.
2. My income-producing abilities are endless.
3. My positive mind is bigger than any obstacle.

Ritual #4

You cannot successfully focus on manifesting abundance
while being ticked off about your financial relationship
with your ex. It will only frustrate you and stifle your creativity. Whenever you find yourself straying from your
abundant mind, use this ritual to quickly evaporate your
negative money thoughts.

Close your eyes and hold an image of the negative
money thought directly in front of your face. Give it color,
sound, texture, temperature, a scent, and blow it up as big
as you can while still keeping it near you. Then, mentally
send that image off to the other side of the room, shrinking
and blurring it, as anything off in the distance would normally appear. Next, create your perfect image of abundance. It could be a picture of you being showered with
thousand-dollar bills, or making the down payment on your
castle, or taking a world cruise. Build that image in the distance where you've just sent the negative one that has now

disappeared altogether. Build the prosperous you, making the picture clearer and clearer, enlarging it and bringing it directly in front of your face until you just know if you opened your eyes, you'd be able to reach out and touch it.

❧ PART 5 ❧

Your Child

"Children tell stories, but in their tales are enfolded many a mystery and moral lesson. Though they may relate many ridiculous things, keep looking in those ruined places for a treasure."
—Rumi

One bright spring day while we were walking home from the park, I told Esprit her father and I were getting divorced. She was, as she often recalls now, "very close to her feet," counting flowers and sharing stories of third grade. She knew something was wrong, although she had pretended with me for weeks that my red eyes were due to a sudden onset of allergies to everything from doorknobs to dry cleaning. When I knelt down and softly delivered the news, she screamed the scream of sheer terror I thought I'd remember for the rest of my life and was devastated for a while. But I resolved to make things work for her. With a lot of talking, crying, handholding and love, things got better, and better, and better.

37. EXPECT THE BEST FROM YOUR CHILD

"All the world is full of suffering, it is also full of over-coming it."
　　　　　　　　　　　　　　　　　　　　　—Helen Keller

When I was pregnant with Esprit, I called her "Spirit" when I "tummy"-talked to her throughout the day, in part because the first time she moved inside me, it felt more like she was power-surfing than lollygagging around in her amniotic sack sucking her thumb, and in part as an affirmation to ensure her a strong spirit. Under the spell of out-of-whack hormones and pregnant divinings, I blissfully decided it would be her legal birth name. Her father, on the other hand, feared that she would have to endure a long life of associations with liquors and ghosts—and possibly end up wedged between "Moonbeam" and "Wave" in her class of 2002 picture. So he tiptoed up to the front desk while I was still in a labor recovery haze and translated her name into French. Weeks later, when I was much more clearheaded, I thanked him for rescuing her from the society of weird-name kids, but I continued to call her Spirit in my heart until she began school.

Seeing how for as long as I can remember I'd heard that children from divorced or dysfunctional homes were more likely to become menaces to society or themselves, after the divorce drama kicked in, I started to call her Spirit again, both as an affirmation and as a prayer.

Granted, I spent the first nine years of my life in a home with an alcoholic father, and the second nine being raised in the projects by a single mom. And yet, as of this writing, I have not done anything for which I could be jailed, institutionalized, or labeled a big-time dud. Am I the exception, or was the expectation wrong? And what of the thousands and thousands of other shining stars in the world who have dismissed familial, environmental, and physical challenges to become happy, healthy, holy, and successful?

Like most normal teenagers, Esprit keeps a messy room, leaves empty containers in the refrigerator, writes a lot of run-on sentences without periods, lives for loud music and malls, and has chronic chore-phobia, with occasional twinges of smart-mouth. I don't attribute any of those short-comings to my divorce. She is also spirited, bright, funny, athletic, and interesting, and I continue to expect the same great things from her that I did the first time I saw her little face. Expect your child to thrive and to create a life she'll also be proud of by:

1. Setting a good example. Are *you* creating an admirable life for yourself?
2. Holding positive images of her in good times and bad.
3. Encouraging excellence.
4. Keeping her personally accountable for responsible behavior, such as homework, manners, chores, and community service.
5. Helping her work through trouble spots.
6. Acknowledging and honoring her strengths.
7. Teaching her to dream big.
8. Loving her a little more each day.

Affirmations

1. I am willing to nourish my child's excellence.
2. My child has a strong, resilient spirit.
3. I am a shining role model for my child.

38. SIMPLIFY YOUR CHILD'S LIFE

Among the biggest gripes I've heard from kids about their divorcing parents is that everything after the divorce changes so quickly and drastically.

- "Mom signed me up for a ton of afterschool stuff. Most days I don't get home until after 7:00 P.M.," says 12-year-old Donald, whose parents recently separated.
- "A couple of months after the divorce, Mom moved us in with her new boyfriend," says 10-year-old Stephanie.
- "It's like one day I woke up and found out my parents were getting a divorce, that my brother and I were getting split between them, and my last name was going to change to my mother's maiden name. And then I had to go to school," says 15-year-old Billy.
- "I don't get to go fishing with Grampa anymore because Mom is mad at Dad," says 6-year-old Russell.

How would you feel if the only life you'd ever known was dismantled with one decision that wasn't even yours to make, and then you were thrust into the new order without so much as a Kleenex? Pretty miserable and disjointed, I imagine. So here are a few ways to simplify the transition for your child:

- Keep big, rash changes to a minimum the first year: reactionary relocations, new schools, romances, names, etc.

- Keep their routines simple, familiar, and manageable.
- Maintain traditions and rituals. These will carry children through the bad times, and make the good times even richer.

Affirmations

1. Simplifying my child's life brings order and comfort.
2. My child thrives in simplicity.
3. When I'm making big decisions, I always think of my child's well-being.

39. Don't Undermine Your Ex's Parenting Skills

I used to wake up in cold sweats during the first visitations, with scary movie music playing in my head and images of Esprit with Don King hair, tranced out in front of the television at her dad's, licking the bottom of an economy-size container of chocolate frosting.

When I asked some other women to share their biggest nightmare worries while their children were spending time with their fathers, I discovered I was not alone.

- *Sarah, 23:* "I worry that my 16-month-old is lying around in a soiled diaper with flies circling while her dad is snoring on the couch."
- *Christina, 29, mother of 4-year-old Seth:* "He doesn't have child-proof locks on his cabinets, and sometimes I picture my little scientist Seth pouring himself a glass of ammonia."
- *Kolina, 31, mother of 6- and 7-year-olds Brett and Ashlee:* "My biggest worry is that he won't watch the kids carefully at the park, and they'll wander off with a stranger."
- *Miriam, 35, mother of 5-year-old twins:* "Sometimes I think he's having sex with his girlfriend while the kids are watching cartoons in the same bed."
- *Elizabeth, 42, mother of 15-year-old Claudia:* "I just know she's on the phone with her girlfriends, from the moment she gets there until the moment she leaves, eating pizza, not doing a lick of homework."

- *Alana, 47:* "I wonder if my 17-year-old son is sharing a beer or a joint with him."

Hygiene, protection, sexual innocence, good nutrition, and a drug- and alcohol-free visit are important, but let me ask you this: Has your child ever returned home from your ex's bloated up like a sumo wrestler, reeking of bodily waste, household cleansers, or reefer, with an afterglow, hangover, or phone-print face, or with reports of the bad man at the park who wanted to take her home and bake her for dinner? Alrighty then.

If anything, you're a wee bit skeptical about Pooh-bah's parenting ideals, you miss your child, and you still hate his guts, no? But it's like this: As squirrelly and unscrupulous as Pooh-bah can be toward you, he probably loves his child, has honorable intentions toward her, and is not the bungling parental idiot you imagine him to be. And if he is, how much damage can he do in a weekend? While you're wondering how I could possibly be so insensitive about his shoveling M&M's into your son's mouth every hour, I'd like to ask you to consider the following three-step, get-a-grip strategy to tide you over until your child comes back home.

Step 1: When you find negative thoughts coming up about your child's "dad" time, use the Cancel, Cancel technique back in Part 1 (page 65).
Step 2: Visualize a positive scene with them, and linger on the moments when your child has returned to you safe, happy, and well cared for.
Step 3: Pamper yourself.

Affirmations

1. I will be the best parent I can be, and allow him to do the same.
2. I trust that my child will always be well cared for.
3. I release my need to criticize my ex's parenting skills.

40. TALK OUT THEIR TROUBLES

This may turn out to be a confusing time in your children's lives, and while you should expect the best from them, be willing to listen, clarify, and alleviate their divorce-related jitters. I've often been able to break most of Esprit's post-divorce troubles down into the following categories:

- *Grown people's business:* "Are we broke?" "Do you think we'll move away from Daddy?" "Who's that man who called for you yesterday?" and other remarks about money, housing, transportation, bills, work, suitors, and other adult responsibilities and activities.
  Tactical responses: Distraction, rhetorical questions, or hopelessly vague, Zen-like statements such as "What is money anyway when I have your love?"
- *Fleeting adolescent worries:* "Will I have to change my name?" "Can I give Dad's phone number out to my friends when I'm at his house?" "Is Dad's brother still my uncle?" "Can I leave some of my books at Dad's?" and other lightweight wonderings.
  Tactical response: "Yes" or "No."
- *Reasonable qualms:* "Dad's girlfriend wants me to call her 'Mom.' Do I have to?" "Why do you think Dad is late

> *"It is no slight thing that those who are so fresh from God, love us."*
> —CHARLES DICKENS

all of the time?" "Do I have to go over to Daddy's this weekend?" "Why'd you get divorced?" and other intricate "well-being" and "mental health" subjects.

Tactical response: When Esprit was smaller, I used moralistic fables or I lied. When she grew older, I turned to metaphors, an abridged version of the truth, and probing, problem-solving questions. Here are a few examples of how you can use these techniques with your child:

1. Your 5-year-old asks you if she'll ever live with Daddy again.
   You say: "Remember Betty Bird in the book we read the other day? She lived with her mommy sometimes and her daddy sometimes. Would you like me to read you that story again?"

2. Your 10-year-old says: "I'd still like to visit my grandma [your ex's mother]. Is that okay with you?"
   You say: "Yes."

3. Your 13-year-old asks: "Do I have to go over to Dad's this weekend? His wife gets on my nerves."
   You say: "Well, honey, you know your dad really enjoys spending time with you. Do you think you could talk to him about it, so the three of you can work something out?"

4. Your 16-year-old asks: "Why did you divorce Dad anyway?"
   Whether you think he's a rodent creep or not, you give some 30-word discourse on one of the following themes: "We grew apart." "We thought it was best." "We tried and tried and it just didn't work out."

Three Other Things to Keep in Mind

1. Do not take your child's momentary spats with her father as an opening to move in and bash him into eter-

nity. She'll forgive him a thousand times, and be thankful, because she'll forgive you at least that many times too.

2. Help your child make light of little troubles too.
3. Teach her to problem-solve by sitting in meditation and using think-alongs, creative play, and role-playing.

Affirmations

1. I enjoy quieting my child's troubled mind.
2. Teaching my child to become a better communicator pleases me.
3. I am comfortable answering my child's questions in a variety of ways.

41. MIND YOUR MOUTH

Nothing will send your children into emotional mayhem faster than a few choice digs from you about their father. Which of the following do you think is the most appropriate response to this question from your child: "Do you hate my dad?"

A. A long, drawn-out dissertation about every sin he's committed against you from the first day you met.
B. "What do you mean by 'hate'?"
C. "Did *he* tell you I hated him?"
D. Silence, with an inquisitive will-she-be-permanently-dysfunctional-if-I-tell-the-truth? look.
E. "No," or some loving question or statement like "How could I possibly hate him when he's part of you?"

You circled E, right? And what if the answer to C is yes, and your ex is baiting you through your child? Journey and playact your way back to E.

Once when Pooh-bah hadn't paid child support for eight months, I arrived home to find a voice mail message from him to Esprit: "Esprit, I left $50 for you in your school office." I replayed the message 10 times, hoping to hear something different. Did he not know that since I paid the phone bill, I was the keeper of voice mail code and that there would be no secret drop-off money messages to Esprit?

Several hours after I'd sedated myself with a warm bath, a fire, and some chamomile tea, and settled down for an episode of *Star Trek,* he called again and asked, "Did Esprit get *her* money today?" Fortunately, Esprit was at basketball practice, so I had an opportunity to explain the fundamentals of child support before "fun" money, and told him I was going to confiscate the money until he took care of his debts. What he said next made me wonder why I hadn't noticed he was loony-tunes when we were married, and if the heckler-me would need a restraining order. "How can you do that?! @#$! Why are you going to punish her because I'm not paying child support?"

I mean, really. Has your ex ever said something so logically faulted, so crazy, that you couldn't explain to him why it's not crazy because he came up with it in the first place? Well, somehow after a little journeying and at least 50 internal repetitions of *"no comprendo inglés"* while he continued to rant, I managed to return to consciousness long enough to go over the child support arrears issue again, and have him hang up on me midsentence. God only knows how much I longed to *69 him and call him a four-headed do-do-brained maggot, but I stoked my fire instead. The phone rang again a half hour later, and because Esprit was out, I answered, knowing it might be Pooh-bah, calling to finish his tirade. It was the blood bank. Could I come in tomorrow to donate?

Esprit, of course, found out about the matter the next time she was over to his place and protested, "Why do I have to suffer? I'm a teenager and I need money, Mom." I silently hugged her and sequestered myself in my room with my Small Thoughts journal.

Underhanded gifts to your child from Pooh-bah, especially a Pooh-bah who doesn't pay child support, might be a sore topic for you. What if Pooh-bah has somehow managed to shower your child with birthday gifts and holiday goodies, even though he hasn't paid child support all year and has driven you into debt and lipstick deprivation? Has his name become synonymous with fun, fast food, and, to quote the comedian Sinbad, "Uncle Daddy," while yours, on the other hand, has been translated to chores and casseroles and "Ole mom"? You are not alone.

- "When my son turned 6, his father dropped off a super-action figure with accessories for his birthday. The thing couldn't have cost more than $30, but the way I waved it in the air and went on about it for two hours, you would have thought I could have taken it back to the store and gotten enough money to take care of all of my bills. I hate that he gets to be the good guy. I gave the toy back to my son and apologized for yelling, but he has never played with it," says Gloria, a 36-year-old who has gone without child support for two years.
- "My ex leaves gifts for our toddler at his parents', who baby-sit sometimes, and tries to make it seem like they bought them, but I know it's him," says 29-year-old Shelly of her newly married ex-husband, who's recently stopped paying child support.
- "He bought our son a new car for his seventeenth birthday. Was that supposed to make up for the four years we've gone without child support because he's been lying about his business being in the red?" says 50-year-old Jillian.

Coping with underhanded gifts when your ex is in arrears is a hard lesson in ex school. But here are some coping strategies:

1. If you have any advance warning of the gift, and it's extravagant, use the Pooh-bah Power Talk with your ex to request an alternative gift, such as child support, or offer a negative consequence, such as confiscating the gift from your child.
2. Take 10 deep breaths and think before you speak if the gift is under $10.

3. Allow amnesty gift-giving periods for birthdays, holidays, or special occasions.

If the gift is abnormally extravagant, such as a car, tell your child that you are going to return it and get him a few other things, and put the rest into the household budget.

You've stopped skywriting insulting remarks about your child's father, or blurting them out in the midst of dinner by now, right? Well, what about the coy or encrypted digs?

See if you recognize your roundabout slamming style below:

- *The Media Slam*—You let the media say it for you.
  Symptoms: You "accidentally" manage to turn on the TV just in time to catch documentaries on deadbeat fathers or talk shows about uncooperative exes, and mistakenly keep picking up *Thelma and Louise* at the movie rental place when your child asks for *Mrs. Doubtfire.*
- *The Bedtime Story Slam*—You let children's writers say it for you through furry little creatures.
  Symptoms: You favor fairy tales in which the mythical dad comes to an untimely or savage end. For example, the squirrel dad gets whisked away by the monkey people, never to be seen again. The mouse dad goes off to find food for his family and gets eaten by a cat.
- *The Indirect Comparison Slam*—You use quotes from friends about their Pooh-bahs to say it for you.
  Symptoms: You make remarks like "Charlee's mother says her dad has the sensitivity of a Chia Pet when he shows up late for visitation." "Donna is thinking about starting a petition to have all deadbeat dads shipped off to Siberia to slew slop."

Please stop. Even though you're not outright saying "I hate your dad," even a 5-year-old can read between the lines. To totally purge yourself of a naughty mouth, practice catching yourself 10 seconds before the offending thought passes your lips, and internally repeat one of the affirmations below several dozen times.

Affirmations

1. I find positive or neutral comments to make about my ex.
2. Mindful silence is an acceptable response.
3. I enjoy preserving my child's mental health.

42. Be Patient During Trying Times

Once I saw a sign that read: "Life is not a series of traumatic events, but a playground of opportunities for grace and growth."

Separation and divorce are such playgrounds, for both you and your child. Sometimes because of divorce and the trials and tribulations of growing up on Planet Earth, your child may appear schizophrenic, bizarre, moody, even downright evil, and unexpectedly strike out at you or your ex. "When William said his dad had crusty toes and looked like Bozo the Clown because he was losing his hair, I happily sat down beside him and added that he hadn't graduated from high school either, and we did the 'bad daddy' dozens for a little while. But when his dad called for him the next day, William asked if he could spend the night," said 40-year-old Jane of her 8-year-old son.

Esprit was mad at Pooh-bah one night during a school candy fundraiser. I didn't know this until I mentioned phoning him to see if he wanted to buy anything for his sweet tooth. "I have no father," she said, walking to her room to retrieve her sales kit and my order form, listing other prospects aloud. "Yes, you do," I said, tagging along behind her to find out what was the matter. "We have seen him." "No, that's the guy you married and had sex with, but I was adopted. Wasn't I? It's okay, you can tell me," she said, twisting her face like she was in between laughter and tears. "No, you weren't adopted," I said. "Do you want me to describe my agonizing 30-hour labor to you again, or do you want to tell me what's going on now?" Apparently, he'd broken a promise and she was in a funk. She too has a very small grudge span, so as we were sailing through the neighborhood later on our bikes, I heard her call out behind me, "Do you think Daddy would like the turtle candy?"

Your kids are going to go through their love-hate cycles with their dad, and with you, for the rest of their lives. Your job is to see them through the waves. Try comforting them with:

- A hug
- A fun or calming activity or ritual
- Pampering
- A soothing talk
- Giving them time to recover on their own

And teach them to be patient with you through your ups and downs.

Thirty-four-year-old Linia sadly admits to saying the following to her 9-year-old daughter one day: " 'I wish I'd never met your dad anyway.' I was so mad at him for not showing up to watch her in her school play that I didn't really think about what implications my remark had at the time about her existence."

When you're hit with a mysterious case of 24-hour dementia and you forget your goddess code of behavior, apologize quickly and do better the next time. My favorite naughty-mouth apology is "Oh my goodness, I can't believe I said something so stupid [bashing myself on the forehead with my palm]. What was I thinking? Was that me? It will never happen again. I'm so sorry."

Affirmations

1. I am a wonderful mother raising a wonderful child.
2. May I grow and deepen to meet my child's needs.
3. I am big enough to apologize and correct myself.
4. Patience becomes me.

43. BUILD A VILLAGE AROUND THEM

Your children, like you, will benefit from a support system now and throughout their lives. Your family and friends may already be an important part of your child's life, sharing fun and educational activities, advising, inspiring, and loving them up, but here are some other people you might want to invite into your child's "village":

- Teachers your child likes and admires, perhaps in his favorite subject, sport, or extracurricular activity
- Members of your church or spiritual family
- Colleagues: coworkers and/or members of professional groups you belong to who you think might enjoy spending time with your child
- Youth leaders: Boy Scout and Girl Scout leaders, Big Brothers and Big Sisters, etc.

Some of these people may already consider themselves "village" members and regularly support your child. Bring others on board by making them part of regular gatherings and outings or shared hobbies.

Affirmations

1. My child is part of a larger village of loving hearts.
2. We're drawing people into our lives to support us.
3. My child is open to receiving love from many places.

Ritual #5

Rituals can help provide a regular source of comfort, balance, and celebration. They can mark milestones in your life and enhance your day-to-day connection with yourself, your child, and others. This exercise is specifically designed to help you develop simple, but enjoyable, daily and weekly rituals with your child. Choose one or more of the ideas below, or create your own, and do them at the same time every day or every week, and cherish this time with your child.

1. *Daily ritual*
   - Dining/preparing a meal
   - Praying
   - Reading or storytelling
   - Sports/exercise
   - Arts and crafts
   - Pampering
   - Singing
   - Games
2. *Weekly ritual*
   - Special at-home meal
   - Movie night
   - Library night
   - Church/spiritual service
   - Dining out
   - Pampering
   - Slumber party
   - Friday-night activity

It's time for a pampering break! Before you continue on, treat yourself to something from your master pampering list.

PART 6

A Few Other Things That Will Help

"It is life near the bone where it is sweetest."
—Thoreau

Once I dreamt I was flying above my entire life, past my birth, my childhood, my young adulthood, my marriage and Esprit's birth, past my divorce and the ensuing drama to a future moment in time. I landed on a sunny mountaintop in my silk pj's, and seven giggling fairies emerged from a nearby cave, draped me in a flowing purple robe, wrapped my head in a soft, fine purple silk turban, and dabbed glitter and gold on my cheeks. Then they formed a procession line and each came skipping forward to hand me a tiny golden slip of paper with one word written on it. The first one said "Love." The next, "Peace." Then, "Faith," "Creativity," "Compassion," Self-mastery." The last fairy, giggling, gave me her slip, "Laughter," and took my hand and led me through the small cave from which they had all come. On the other side, I stepped out into a beautiful, beautiful paradise alive with friends, music, and laughter.

44. MAKE SURE YOU GET PRINCE CHARMING THE NEXT TIME

"So many new friends arrive when we stop making love to enemies." —Marianne Williamson

After watching a talk show, a friend called to report that she was adopting one of the guest's mottoes when it came to new romantic possibilities: "When you see ugly coming, cross the street." Next time you see a man who looks like, sounds like, and behaves like Pooh-bah headed your way, cross the street, *and run*. Now, I could sit here and say I was hypnotized and drugged when I married Pooh-bah, or that he went through a major personality change during our marriage. But I'm sitting next to a mammoth tree right now and I don't want any "freak" accidents, if you know what I mean.

Surely, I didn't know the extremes to which he would mutate, but I knew he was an eccentric, moody, remarkably stubborn, near-chain-smoking, couch dweller who didn't like to pay bills and often pointed out that God spelled backward was "dog." In my defense, I was young and sprung, and like many young brides, I thought I'd just change the things I didn't like two weeks after the wedding. So when he asked me to marry him for the fifth time, I wistfully said yes. And in 7+ years, we had many sweet moments and artistic collaborations—including our "Golden Child"—but our love boat eventually turned into the *Titanic*.

After a man-fast, determined to redeem myself in the "love" arena, I wrote the following God-letter two years after our divorce:

Dear God,

I'd like a single, well-read, height and weight proportionate, joyful, mellow, kind, gentle (yet manly), bright, funny, sensual, well-mannered, considerate, communicative, courageous, healthy, visionary, creative, attentive, romantic, responsible, dependable, strong, evolved, spiritual, charismatic, kindred man with nice teeth and facial hair. I'm willing to wait a lifetime for him, but if by some chance you could drop him off on my doorstep tomorrow noon, that would be just fine too.

Thank you,

Nailah

Year 6, my king and I collided at a bookstore. But I didn't know he was mine until we'd been platonic spiritual friends for a year or so, sharing our dates-from-hell-and-beyond stories as well as thoughts on many of the things we still talk about most every day—books, joy, health, metaphysics, creativity, family, and the workings of the human mind. Then we enrolled in a hypnotherapy training program, a mutual lifetime goal, neither of us planning to fall into the ultimate trance, love. But if you knew him, you'd understand. He's the man in the letter and I love him to the heavens. But enough about my kindred, here are two writing exercises to help you clarify what you want in a new love and to draw him into your life if he isn't there already.

Exercise 1: Describe Him

First, take a few minutes to study your writings from the release exercise in Chapter 9, "Reduce Your Ex Cooties," where you listed the things you desired most from your ex. Do you want them from a future intimate? Next, close your eyes, and create a picture of *him* in your mind. What does he look like? What are his interests and personality traits?

What else about him lets you know that he's "the one"?
Now, describe him in the space below.

_____

_____

_____

_____

_____

Exercise 2: Write Him a Letter

Close your eyes again and pretend for a moment that
you've just ended a perfect day with the man of your
dreams and that he is sitting next to you right now holding
you in his arms. On the table before you is a letter that
you've written earlier in the day spilling over with gratitude
for the many ways he's blessed your life and your child's.
In your mind's eye, imagine yourself reaching for that letter now, opening it, and reading it aloud to him. Now, open
your eyes, get a few sheets of paper and an envelope, and
write the contents of that imaginary letter, in present tense,
on your paper. Then seal the letter, and if your love is in
your life, give it to him. If he's not, tuck the letter away for
safekeeping and deliver it when it's time.

Affirmations

1. Every day, I grow and become a better me.
2. I'm ready to meet the man of my dreams.
3. I deserve a wonderful life partner.

45. Take a Bow and Keep Growing

Your true success has little to do with whether your ex is still imitating one of the Three Stooges or not. Measure it instead by the ground you've gained on the goals you set for yourself when you mapped out your sanity plan (pages 20–25). Are you feeling more powerful? More graceful? More in control of your emotions? Does your Small Thoughts journal feel neglected? Or better yet, have you replaced it by now with a Big Thoughts journal?

By and by, the quest after you've met one set of goals, celebrated, and rested is to then go on and become something more. What are you going to do with the rest of your life now that you're over this Pooh-bah thing? Only you know. One of the ways I answer this question for myself is by creating short-term and long-term personal growth themes for myself. For example, this year I immersed myself for one month in juicing, hiking, advanced yoga, vitamin therapy, and so on. Another month, my theme was to massage Esprit's feet every day. Another month, I attended evening classes at the local Herb Farm and came a few baby steps closer to becoming a master herbalist. Another month, since I hide out when I'm writing, I filled my calendar with "special time" appointments with each of my friends. Another month, I made arrangements to exchange cooking lessons with a workmate who was Indian. I taught her Thai Cuisine, she taught me Indian. When I finish this book, I imagine I'll go to the mountains or the beach for a bit, and then dive into my next goal. List 10 things you would like to accomplish in the next three months, the next year, and the next three years:

Next 3 Months   **Next Year**   **Next 3 Years**

_____

_____

_____

_____

_____

_____

_____

_____

_____

Affirmations

1. I'm proud to walk the high road.
2. My life is delicious.
3. I enjoy filling my days with new adventures.

46. If You Get Off Track, Get Back On

True to my word, I never had another lapse of pretend voodoo priestess, but because I lived this book while writing it, I did have a few other dark nights in the past seven years, one of which in particular stands out in my mind.

You-know-who developed a new strain of irritating behavior about five years A.D., and I went to work with my affirmations and prayers, mailed myself a dozen love notes, doubled up on Yanni and Gabrielle Roth tapes, and none of it worked. A weary goddess, I drove over to Alma's for moral support and intervention, and I believe my exact words when she opened the door were "Damn the high road, girl. Do you suppose it's possible to make a jump rope out of someone's intestines and keep them alive long enough so they could watch you jumping rope with it?" *Really.*

She silently led me into her den, put my feet in a vibrating foot tub, and dripped sedating essential oils into the tub as she massaged my hands and lovingly pierced holes in all of my Pooh-bahcide scenarios and alibis. She also suggested that I could be wrong about God's hearing problem; that I wasn't being ignored, I was being strengthened and given what I wanted in an intriguing roundabout way so I could be an inspiration to others. And when I said I wasn't going to finish the book, she calmly said, "Okaaaaaaaaaaaaaaay . . ."—she really dragged it out too—and minutes later after more oils and soft strokes, she said, "Of course you're going to finish it. You have to. This is yours to do. And put this in there too so they know sucky moments pass."

And I cried and called her a liar until her love, the soothing water, and the oils lifted my despair, and I was ready to go out and face the cold, cruel world again with a warm heart.

Try not to sweat your dark nights too much. They'll come and go, sometimes in multiples, and you might think you're dying, but what you're doing is too big to come without a few slips and slides. Have your breakdowns, and then your breakthroughs, and allow that very process of contracting and expanding to help you grow. I believe that angels hold us while we sleep and hover beside us when we're working, playing, and going about our lives. And I believe that when we are in our darkest nights, they slip inside us and help us do what we think we cannot. *So hold on.* Ask your angels and your family for help through the waves, pray, wait, learn, look around for signs and wonders, and do not be daunted by the rhythm. *It will pass.* Try these other "dark night" strategies:

- Have a Day Without Words, with lots of altar time and affirmations, and count your blessings.
- Pamper, pamper, pamper.
- Exercise.
- Review your strategies and mentally revisit better days.
- Keep the faith and expect something wonderful to follow every dark night.

Affirmations

1. I'm pleased with myself, and I celebrate who I am.
2. I patiently love and support myself at all times.
3. I am a light in the darkness.

47. Get More Help If You Need It

So far, I've talked a lot about putting your life back in order with humor, self-care, emotion management, power communication, prayer, creativity, and strategizing. For many of you, for most of this journey, these ideas will be plenty. But, if there's ever a time in your life you look in the mirror and the lizard-tail lady is staring back at you, I want you to consider professional counseling. Although I became a registered counselor shortly before this book was published, and I may be diminishing my own income by saying this, I want you to keep in mind that you are always directly responsible for your own glory. Counseling can provide week-to-week emotional support and wonderful strategies, but you still have to do the work of managing your life.

Counseling

If I were your counselor, on your first visit, I would collect background information and find out what's currently going on in your life. Then I'd ask you what you wanted your life to look like. If that vision was reasonable (i.e., you weren't asking me to help you get back home to Saturn), in subsequent visits, I'd help you remove negative behaviors and emotions that were keeping you from that life. I would also often send you home with exercises and tools to support you in making those changes. If you believe you

could benefit from counseling, here are some tips to help
you find a counselor in your area:

1. Before you start your search for a counselor, access
   your own needs and set your own goals. Make a list
   of 10 things you want to get out of counseling and
   how you think a counselor can help you.
2. Ask friends who've grown from counseling for referrals.
3. Meet with the counselor for one to three sessions.
   After that, if you decide she's not a good "fit," find
   someone else. If she is, cooperate and be honest
   about what's going on in your life and what you are
   willing to do in your own behalf.
4. Think of her as your "wellness" partner.

Affirmations

1. Asking for help is a brave, loving act.
2. I'm in charge of my recovery.

48. CREATE YOUR OWN AFFIRMATIONS

Some people regard affirmations as lies, grand mal delusions, and sheer craziness, but I like to think of them, like playacting, as motivational tools that can carry us to a brighter place. I want you to try a little experiment right now. Put your book down, grit your teeth, and say to yourself internally or out loud 25 times, "I'm an awful person." Believe me, you have no idea how many people do this thousands of times a day, or something equally self-defeating. How motivating do you think these internal attacks are? For example, do you think someone who's constantly running around thinking she's awful is positioning herself for greatness? Or do you think she's going to wake up the next day and start the dread songs all over again? If your mind is going to gravitate toward thoughts—and we have thousands of them every day—why can't they be positive thoughts?

Throughout the book, I've provided you with many affirmations to recondition your mind to flow toward the positive. I hope you will use them often, and more so, I hope you take them a step forward and create your own, as the situations require. The more you learn to affirm the good throughout your days, the more everything else will fall to the background and blur. So here are a few tips to help you create your own affirmations:

- Make them positive and short.
- Recite them in the present tense, as if they're happening now.

- Repeat them at least 25 times a sitting, several times a day. Limit yourself to one to three affirmations a day.
- If it's a particularly hard-to-believe affirmation to counter something that normally makes you sad or crazed in the head, recite it in front of a mirror.

Practice Writing Affirmations

In order to get the feel of how affirmations are written, compose your own affirmations for the following dilemmas:

1. Anxiety or dread about talking to your ex
2. Feelings of aloneness
3. Feelings of victimization
4. Anxiety about your child going to visit your ex
5. Money worries

Now that you have written your own, examine these suggestions for each of the above problems:

1. I am able to communicate easily with my ex.
2. I'm open to drawing strength from people who love me.
3. I am willing to grow through this.
4. I am comfortable with my child spending time with her father.
5. Money and abundance flow into my life.

Affirmations

1. I enjoy reprogramming my mind to think most positively.
2. I am learning to look for the silver lining more often.
3. My mind is capable of beautiful thoughts.
4. I insist on being happy and fulfilled.

49. WRITE A THANK-YOU LETTER TO YOUR EX

Okay, okay, stop hyperventilating for a moment and let me explain myself. Can you pretend again with me for a moment that you don't think Pooh-bah was really sent to drive you to the edge of madness, as you did at the beginning of this book? What if he really was your teacher? Well, now that you've mastered the strategies in this book and you're about to graduate from the seven kinds of fresh hell he's put you through, in the spirit of good manners and gratitude, it's time for that thank-you note.

So go get a piece of paper. *Go on*. First, take a few moments to wander back to your answers for *High Road Jeopardy!* in Chapter 1, which are all valid things to thank Pooh-bah for. You might also want to add anything that came up in the course of reading this book, and also thank him for your child, for once being a loving part of your life, and for preparing you for a more fulfilling relationship in the future. Now, write, and when you finish the letter, seal it and place it on your altar for a few days and then tuck it away in a special hideaway place.

Affirmations

1. I express gratitude to all of my teachers.
2. I release through thanksgiving.

50. BUILD A
MEMORABLE LIFE

*"Far away, there in the sunshine are my highest as-
pirations. I may not reach them, but I can look up
and see their beauty, believe in them, and try to follow where they lead."* —Louisa May Alcott

Now that I'm almost on the last page of this book, you
should know that my life was a three-ring circus from page
one on. There was Pooh-bah in ring one, being Pooh-bah.
Esprit, in ring two, in a puberty stranglehold, and my
mother, whose health had deteriorated into the danger
zone, in ring three. And I kept writing through bizarre
Pooh-bah and teenage dramas, and new dynamics of parent care *like you would not believe,* as well as through ordinary qualms over what to fix for dinner, carpooling,
homework, PMS, counting couch change, and deciding
whether or not to let my hair grow out. I kept writing because I saw the good this book could bring, and because,
quite frankly, every time I tried to stop writing it, God
would not let me be. God, as you may know by now, is a
master nagger, and when you do not do the things She's as-
signed you, She really knows how to get in your face.

This was also one of the most delicious times in my life.
I fell in love with the king I plan to marry, watched Esprit
blossom into a young lady, deepened my friendships,
played in the snow with my older nephews and practically
melted when I held the newest one for the first time, took
100 Saturdays' worth of cooking and health classes, built a
new career for myself, ran a campaign, cooked meals for
the homeless, ran back down Tiger Mountain 100 times,
took a million lavender baths, and parasailed. Which set of
adventures do you think I'm celebrating most right now?

Someone once told me a story of a squirrel who'd been regularly eating out of a man's birdfeeder. The man was delighted when the squirrel came to feast, but he apparently didn't know the squirrel favored sunflower seeds, and he decided to give him some variety by filling up the feeder with a new seed and grain mixture, with only 10 percent sunflower seeds. The man returned the morning after he'd made the switch to find the sunflower seeds eaten and the rest sprawled on the ground. *Do that with your life.* Hold your head up high, be powerful and graceful, cherish yourself, and create a beautiful life for yourself and your child. Feast on your sunflower seeds, and fling the rest to the ground. And keep your belly and your heart full of the wonder of that life. God bless you, and may the laugh be with you.

Affirmations

1. My life is my own to design.
2. Every moment, I'm choosing to create a wonderful life.
3. I inspire myself.

> *"There is nothing left to you at this moment but to have a good laugh."*   —Zen master

Ritual #6

I began this book by telling you to embrace the challenges with your ex as an opportunity to become something more, and I want to end it in this closing ritual by giving you a vivid glimpse of that something more. Find a comfortable chair or lie down on your bed or the floor where you will not be disturbed. Relax your body by counting backward from 25 to 1, breathing in a very relaxed manner. With each breath, you will feel more and more relaxed. Really let go, and notice how it feels to relax each muscle of your body. When you reach the number 1, imagine yourself in your favorite place six months from now, wearing your favorite thing, surrounded by your favorite people, or all alone but content and totally relaxed and happy, doing exactly what you want to do. Breathe in the spirit of this image, really feeling the weight of the clothes you're wearing, the colors all around you, the faces, if there are any, of the people who love you. Magnify the sound of their voices, or the soft breeze of your own silence, and enjoy, enjoy, enjoy.

Bibliography: Other Books You May Want to Read During This Crazy Time in Your Life

The Art of Selfishness—David Seabury, Cornerstone Library (Simon & Schuster), 1937.

The Artist's Way: A Spiritual Path to Higher Creativity—Julia Cameron, Jeremy P. Tarcher/Perigee, 1992.

The Healing Power of Humor: Techniques for Getting Through Loss, Setbacks, Upsets, Disappointments, Difficulties, Trials, Tribulations, and All That Not-So-Funny Stuff—Allen Klein, Jeremy P. Tarcher, Inc., 1989.

How to Talk So Kids Will Listen & Listen So Kids Will Talk—Adele Faber and Elaine Mazlish, Avon Books, 1980.

I'm on My Way but Your Foot Is on My Head—Beatrice Berry, Ph.D., Simon & Schuster, 1996.

Living Juicy: Daily Morsels for Your Creative Soul—Sark, Celestial Arts, 1994.

Living Your Life Out Loud—Salli Rasberry and Padi Selwyn, Pocket Books, 1995.

The Magic of Thinking Big—David J. Schwartz, Ph.D., Prentice-Hall Inc., 1959, 1965.

Practical Intuition—Laura Day, Villard, 1996.

Simplify Your Life: 100 Ways to Slow Down and Enjoy the Things that Really Matter—Elaine St. James, Hyperion, 1994.

You Can Heal Your Life—Louise L. Hay, Hay House, 1984.

ABOUT THE AUTHOR

Nailah Shami, aka "Esprit's mom," is the originator and director of the *National Get Along with Your Ex Campaign*. She is also a certified aromatherapist, a Reiki master, a registered counselor in the state of Washington, and a certified clinical hypnotherapist specializing in personal growth and wellness. To order relaxation, motivational, and personal growth audiotapes, or for more information about the *National Get Along with Your Ex Campaign,* write to:

PMB #191 15127 N.E. 24th Street,
Redmond, WA 98052-5547